The Illustrated Library of

NATURE

VOLUME 1

ANIMAL
TRAITS

The American Museum of Natural History

Cooperated in the publication of this edition.

The opinions expressed by authors are their own and do not necessarily reflect the policy of the Museum.

The Illustrated Library of
NATURE

𝒯HIS PICTORIAL ENCYCLOPEDIA of natural history and ecology depicts the
relationships of all living organisms to each other and between
them and their environments. Original manuscript from the
Doubleday Nature Programs plus new articles and illustrations are included in this edition.

H. S. STUTTMAN CO., INC., Publishers
New York, N.Y., 10016

Introduction

ON THIS VAST and wondrous planet we call Earth over a million species of animals and over 350,000 different species of plants have been identified and described. Naturalists estimate that millions of other ones have yet to be discovered

The human family is but a single species amidst this enormous variety of living things. Yet man's position is unique, for he is both a participant and a spectator. Because all of nature—which includes every form of life on the globe—is a great unity, and all the parts are related one to the other, our careful observations can reveal much more than the mere details of what goes on in the world around us; they can illuminate as well our own activities and feelings, clarify our thinking and deepen our understanding. If in addition our approach is one of respect and appreciation, there is no telling what secrets nature may unfold to us or where those unlocked doors may lead.

In this *Illustrated Library of Nature* we have endeavored to bring the reader a vivid, colorful and accurate record of the natural life that inhabits the land, air and waters which surround and support us. In so doing we also hoped to share some of the accumulated wealth of knowledge that naturalists have gathered and to portray throughout the harmonious interrelationship of all living things. The fact, for example, that some animals prey on others is not an indication of discord in nature; on the contrary, it is simply a part of that intricate network of activities by which the natural world is maintained and kept in balance. It is for the reader who delights in exploring all the untold facets of this many-hued and splendid picture that these volumes have been planned. They were not intended as a text for a structured curriculum in natural history.

In order to fulfill the twin purposes of clarity and reading enjoyment, we have categorized the material within a meaningful and orderly framework which, however, is not overly-rigid in presentation. Consequently, there is sufficient latitude in the organization to allow each writer to explore related questions and phenomena that shed light on, and enhance the interest of, the particular area he is illustrating. To

facilitate selection, the 57 chapters are grouped in subject areas that are arranged in alphabetical sequence, such as Animal Traits, Animal World, Birds, Cave Life, Desert Life and so forth. Each chapter is virtually a book in itself and, because of its thoroughness and range, may serve as a topical encyclopedia. Moreover, since there is a necessary interrelationship between topics that fall within different subject classifications, the Index will be useful both to the student and to the general reader motivated by his own curiosity and the joy of learning something new.

The pages that follow are filled with more than 3000 illustrations, selected not only for their pictorial accuracy and appropriateness but for their graphic beauty as well. Among these are brilliant camera studies which were produced in the field by some of the world's most prominent nature photographers and which are distributed liberally throughout the text. In addition there are 1389 of the internationally famous wildlife stamps, drawn from life with full attention to all details, color as well as habitat, proportion and form. Text, pictures and story captions live together, so that they complement, enliven and enlarge upon each other.

Our concern with the whole field of natural life called for the participation of a great many experts, while the need for complete, reliable and up-to-date material dictated that these be well-trained, highly skilled and talented individuals. Most of the contributors represented here were the authors, illustrators and photographers who created the DOUBLEDAY NATURE PROGRAM. They are renowned, fully qualified specialists in their subjects. Among them are eminent biologists, botanists, entomologists, ichthyologists, microbiologists, ornithologists and zoologists. The fresh and lively approach they brought to their topics is additional evidence of their outstanding abilities.

If the *Illustrated Library of Nature* is thus the work of many skilled and patient hands, its real value, and its glory, lies in the subject alone —the world of nature. It will be sufficient satisfaction to the publishers if they have succeeded in awakening the reader to the magnificence of this great web of life, which depends so much on us, and upon which we all depend for survival on the earth's thin crust.

Publishing Staff

Editorial Consultant   Alfred Meyer
Editor, Natural History Magazine

Associate Editor   Peter Betcher

Photo Editor   Maureen Gardella

Design   Margot L. Wolf

Contributors

R. Tucker Abbot
Robert Porter Allen
William Hopkins Amos
Herbert R. Axelrod
Alfred M. Bailey
Maurice Burton
W. T. Davidson
Joseph A. Davis
Joseph A. Davis, Jr.
Carroll Lane Fenton
C. A. W. Guggisberg
Russell Gurnee
J. A. Hancock
Bill and Mary V. Hood
Jane S. Kinne
Russ Kinne

Alexander B. Klots
Elsie B. Klots
Robert S. Lemmon
Gertrude I. McWilliams
Edwin A. Menninger
Charles R. Meyer
Charles E. Mohr
Bryan Patterson
Alfred Renfro
L. M. P. Small
Michael F. W. Tweedie
Howard Uikle
Roman Vishniac
Lewis Wayne Walker
Ann Woodlin
Louis Zara

Contents

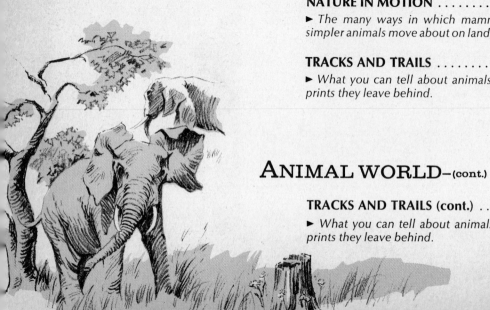

BIRDS

VOLUME 4

BIRDS–(cont.)

CAVE LIFE

VOLUME 5

DESERT LIFE

DUNE LIFE

VOLUME 6

DUNE LIFE–(cont.)

FOREST AND MEADOW LIFE

VOLUME 7

FOREST AND MEADOW LIFE–(cont.)

FRESHWATER LIFE

INSECTS

VOLUME 8

INSECTS–(cont.)

MAMMALS

VOLUME 9

MAMMALS–(cont.)

NATURE HOBBIES

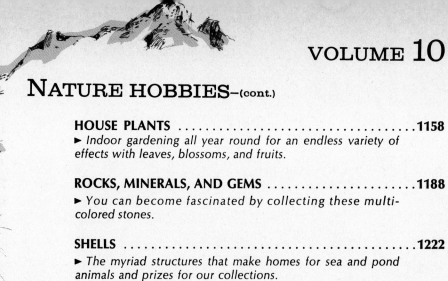

VOLUME 10

NATURE HOBBIES—(cont.)

OCEAN LIFE

VOLUME 11

OCEAN LIFE—(cont.)

VOLUME 12

OCEAN LIFE—(cont.)

PREHISTORIC LIFE

VOLUME 15

PREHISTORIC LIFE–(cont.)

REPTILES AND AMPHIBIANS

SPRINGTIME

WILDLIFE

VOLUME 16

WILDLIFE–(cont.)

WHEN IT IS POSSIBLE to observe the behavior of animals living in their natural state, we discover some remarkable things indeed. Making a home, raising children, getting food and avoiding or defending themselves against enemies are common activities in the life of most animals.

Animals are builders, and in NATURE'S ARCHITECTS we examine their building accomplishments with examples ranging from the lowly, one-celled animal through bees, spiders, birds and mammals. Although many animals get their materials from their own bodies, others collect what they need from their surroundings. Curiously, some of the simplest animals, including some protozoans, are expert architects, while many higher animals, such as apes and monkeys, show little interest in making anything and are rather careless about it when they do.

ANIMAL CHILDREN explores the period between the birth of animals and the time they are able to go off on their own. Not all animals have childhoods, but those that cannot look out for themselves and those that need special training are usually cared for, protected and taught by their parents—or at least their mothers—when they are young. This section includes a variety of examples of child-rearing and also demonstrates how animals learn by imitation, "supervised" play and encouragement.

In the struggle to obtain food and avoid being eaten, nature has supplied animals with a special aid: the ability to conceal themselves by camouflage and play tricks on their opponents. A baby fawn, for example, may be "invisible" to some animal that is looking right at it; or, having crept up unnoticed, a member of the cat family suddenly pounces on its victim. CAMOUFLAGE IN NATURE illustrates the countless "disappearing acts" that animals perform and explains the basic rules that these disguises follow.

In WEAPONS we take a look at the "arms" and devices animals use to defend themselves against attack and to catch and kill what they need to eat. Most animals use bluff—often just a lot of noise—when in danger and some have nothing to back it up. On the other hand a great many can make use of one or more weapons, such as sharp teeth, claws, beaks, poisons, stings, and so on. While considering this fascinating array, however, we should bear in mind that animals in general are peaceful and use their weapons only for survival.

ANIMAL TRAITS

Nature's Architects

IN A MODERN SOCIETY an architect is a highly-skilled person who, as a result of years of training, knows more about buildings and building construction than the rest of us. It may seem inappropriate therefore to speak of animal architects until we recall that the original meaning of the name indicated no more than the chief builder, and that the title can be used also, in a broader sense, for anyone who makes or constructs something. It is only in this last sense that the name can be applied to animals; and in this sense all animals are architects because all (except those that are parasitic) make something. To define our terms of reference, therefore, a brief explanation is necessary.

Two Methods of Building

THERE ARE WORMS which, while related to earthworms, live only in the sea. They are known as marine bristle-worms, to emphasize not only the nature of their habitat but that they have many more bristles than an earthworm. In fact, these extra bristles form a crown or fan on the head, which is used among other things as a drag-net, for most bristle-worms live on small particles of living matter strained from the sea. Their method of gaining a livelihood requires no active life, no rapid movement from place to place, only a shelter from which the worm, when hungry, can push out its crown of bristles and sieve food from the surrounding water. The shelter takes the form of a tube which the bristle-worm itself constructs.

There are two ways in which bristle-worms can make the tube in which it shelters. One way is to give out from its body the lime salts it has taken into its tissues, from its food or from the sea-water. Some bristle-worms do not do even this, but secrete a mucus

In building their homes, animals often make use of the materials that nature provides. Gathering the things they need and placing them in position may require some hard labor and considerable skill. The **parula warbler** of North America (in photograph above, right) makes its work easier by selecting a tuft of lichen known as "Old Man's Beard" for a nesting site.

or slime from the body, which hardens to form a membranous or jelly-like tube. The other way of making a tube is to build it of sand-grains. The worm traps, with its bristles, sand-grains suspended in the surrounding water. Each grain is passed down the bristles to the mouth, taken in the lips, moistened with saliva, and placed in position on the rim of the growing tube. A rough analogy would be to think of a bricklayer standing inside a circular tower which he is building around himself.

Both the worm that builds a limy, or mucous, tube and the one that builds a tube of sand-grains are making something. To that extent both are entitled to be called architects. But the one secretes the material of the tube from its own tissues, just as our own bodies secrete the materials for our bones, or a mollusk secretes its shell. By contrast, the other kind of bristle-worm, which builds a sandy tube around itself, engages in a form of manual labor, in that it picks up materials already formed and places them in position. To do this work the bristle-worm must select the materials it needs, and it must have some manipulative skill to place them in position. Both the selectivity of the worm as well as its manipulative skill may be very slight but they do exist. Even if we say that both are instinctive and require no learning or training, the fact remains that they exist.

As between the worm building a limy or mucous tube and one making a tube of separate sand-grains, we are justified in saying that the first is not a natural architect and that the second is an architect. There is, in fact, a considerable gulf between the methods and the achievements of the two worms, and this gulf is even more marked in the achievements of certain single-celled animals.

Building by a Single Cell

THE SINGLE-CELLED ANIMAL most familiar to us is the amoeba. Its body is naked: that is, it is a single unit of protoplasm with only a membrane clothing it. We are also familiar with the way the amoeba moves about by throwing out rootlike extensions of its body.

(bottom, left)
The **shipworm,** a mollusk with a long, extended body, burrows in timbers submerged in the sea, including those of wooden ships. First the larva settles on the surface of the wood and then, with two shells on the front of its body, it rasps tunnels through the wood, always working along the grain.

(bottom, center)
Bagworms are really moths. The caterpillar clothes itself with fragments of the plants on which it feeds, building a protective bag inside of which it changes to a chrysalis. The female moths never leave this bag, the males having to seek them out and mate with them while they are still inside.

(bottom, right)
The **paper nautilus** is related to squids and octopuses but swims freely in the sea. It has no shell like that of the pearly nautilus, but if she is mated the female makes a paper-thin white shell for her eggs. This is secreted and fashioned by two of her arms which are much enlarged and flattened.

(left)
The **nautilus** is a mollusk with a many-chambered, pearly white shell. As it grows it adds new chambers, or rooms, and moves out of the old ones. The animal itself lives only in the outermost chamber.

CHADER

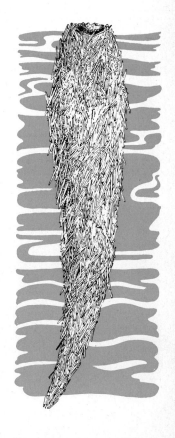

There are, however, other single-celled animals, related to the amoeba, that secrete shells around their bodies, made either of lime or silica. They fashion these in the same way as the bristle-worms make tubes of lime or mucus, by giving out from their bodies materials in solution. In addition, there are yet other single-celled animals that clothe themselves with sand-grains or other small materials lying on the sea-bed. These they pick up with rootlike extensions of their bodies, similar to those of an amoeba, and place them in position around the body. More importantly, the grains are not only selected for size but are so placed in position around the body that their edges fit into each other exactly, to form a mosaic. Indeed, some of these single-celled animals, although only microscopic in size, fashion their coats of sand-grains or other materials so adroitly that at one time the scientists studying them used to speak of the work of these minuscule animals as intelligent.

All this has a very significant bearing on the subject of animal architects, for no one is going to say that a single cell can show intelligence. Yet no one can deny that a single cell is capable of being able to select its building materials and place them with precision so that they exactly fit. And, it must be reiterated, whether we say the work is instinctive or whether we use any other term to describe how it comes about, the basic fact remains that building and building construction among animals is not necessarily associated with a high level of mental capacity. This is not to deny that a high level of architectural attainment is often achieved.

At this point another aspect of this subject must be examined. We have considered three types of single-celled animals. The first, the amoeba, makes nothing, so that its body is naked and it has no skeleton. The second lays down a shell, which is an external skeleton, although in some species it may be internal. The third type actually clothes itself with materials already in existence and which lie, ready to be used, outside the body.

Some of the one-celled protozoans build a covering for themselves by cementing together grains of sand and other available particles, which is more economical than manufacturing the materials themselves. This **foraminifer** has used sponge spicules to build its "home."

(right)
These glistening white skeletons of beautifully interwoven silica threads are superior to human construction, yet each was built by a mere sponge, the **Venus' flower-basket.** Sponges stand at the lowest level in the animal kingdom and their cells, though they can work together, are practically independent of each other.

(above)
The soft, elastic skeleton of the **common sponge** makes it useful in the home for bathing and cleaning. When it is alive, water flows in and out through the many holes, or pores, bringing it food and air. Like all sponges, it is really a colony of single-celled animals that co-operate at times to perform certain important functions, and it possesses only the simplest nervous tissue. This type is usually found in the Mediterranean and the seas around Florida.

Some external skeletons look very like architectural achievements. Indeed, so do some internal skeletons. Among the more familiar "natural works" are the shells made by mollusks and it may well be asked why these should not be included here. The distinction is a fine one, as will be shown by the next example.

The Efficiency of Sponges

SPONGES STAND at the lowest level in the animal kingdom. They are, in their organization, little better than a colony of single-celled animals. They have only the simplest nervous tissue, so simple that at one time it was thought they had no nerve-cells at all. Added to this, the cells in their tissues seem to act independently of each other, and yet, by striking contrast, at times they show the highest degree of co-operation with each other, with the result that they achieve a superlative degree of building construction. This reaches a peak in the sponge known as the Venus' flower-basket.

This is a sponge that lives at a depth of 100 fathoms off the Philippines. In the second half of last century visitors to the Far East used to bring home a Venus' flower-basket as a natural curiosity or as a souvenir of their visit. This sponge is anything up to a foot long and in appearance it looks very like the old-fashioned gas-mantle. When its flesh is dead and washed away there is left a glistening white skeleton of silica threads so beautifully interwoven that a professor of civil engineering once described the skeleton of a Venus' flower-basket as "the finest example of engineering construction". It is a mass of girder-and-strut work, combining the greatest efficiency with the minimum of material. It is superior to any girder-work man can achieve because in addition to its strength and rigidity it is not without resilience or a certain degree of elasticity.

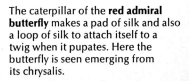

The caterpillar of the **red admiral butterfly** makes a pad of silk and also a loop of silk to attach itself to a twig when it pupates. Here the butterfly is seen emerging from its chrysalis.

This remarkable work is made by the sponge secreting the long slender needles of silica, in the way the bristle-worm secretes its limy tube or the single-celled animal secretes its shell. There is a big difference, however: the cells that secrete the needles of silica in the sponge later transport these needles and place them in the position where they will be most effective. And all this is done by cells virtually independent of each other, yet able to work in concert, in a body that is totally devoid of intelligence and has, at best, only a minimal nervous control.

It is clear that in the Venus' flower-basket the two methods seen in bristle-worms, and in single-celled animals, are combined. The needles are secreted by the tissues, but they are also manipulated and placed in position. This emphasizes how very thin is the line

(left)
In spring the **Pacific giant salamander** burrows at the base of a spring emptying into a stream to create an underground pool. In this it mates, the female lays her eggs and the larvae spend the remainder of the summer.

(below and bottom, left)
Among many wasps, the queen and later the workers chew pieces of wood from posts and trees and turn them to paper, which they use to build their nests. These two photos show views of the interior and exterior of a nest of the **white-faced hornet,** a large wasp.

(bottom, right)
Worker bees produce tiny plates of wax from their bodies to make the cells of the **honeycomb.** The cells are filled with honey and then sealed with more wax. Note that the cells are six-sided, or hexagonal, which not only hold more than triangular or square cells would but are stronger as well.

dividing the two processes. All the same, unless we are to become hopelessly involved in the intricacies of animal physiology and the behavior of animal cells and tissues, it will be as well to make a very clear distinction between those animals that secrete their skeletons and those that build by selection and manipulation.

A sea-shell is a marvelous piece of construction but it is laid down by cells secreting the lime salts. It is no more wondrous than any other skeleton. The masses of white coral left when a stony coral is denuded of its flesh is also marvelous to contemplate, but it also is no more remarkable than our own bones, hair or finger-nails and is laid down in much the same way.

The Work of Bees and Wasps

THE HONEYCOMB made by bees in a hive is no more remarkable but its genesis is different, because the wax of which it is made is manipulated, and although it is akin to the building of the skeleton of the Venus' flower-basket it is the result of a manipulation and, more importantly, the bees that make it can go away and leave it.

We are better informed about what takes place when a honeycomb is built than we are about most other animal architecture because there has been so much research into the behavior of bees. Briefly, a worker produces tiny plates of wax from her body to fashion the cells in which the honey is stored. The wax is laid layer by layer on the wall of the cell until a required height is reached. Then the cell is filled with honey and its opening is sealed with more wax. The question then arises: how does the bee know when fresh cells should be built?

The answer is that there is an automatic control. The forager bees bring pollen and nectar to the hive and pass it to household bees, those concerned with the work inside the hive. These take the pollen and nectar into their stomachs and convert it to honey. When there

is insufficient space in a comb to store the honey the household bee manufacturing it must retain the excess honey in her stomach. When this happens she starts to assimilate some of the sugar into her own system. By the time she has assimilated more than can be used up in her own output of energy, certain glands in her body secrete the excess as wax, the plates of wax coming out between the segments of her abdomen.

All this takes place in the hive and is difficult for the ordinary person to observe, but anyone can see a parallel process at work by watching one of the bees or wasps that use mud or clay, or by watching a queen wasp when she is starting to lay the foundations of a nest. In our picture of the organ-pipe wasp we see the lines of growth on the cells made of mud, where each fresh layer has been added. Bumblebees also make small "honey-pots" which look like miniature clay pots, and there is a great variety of "pots" produced by the various species of bees and wasps. But all have this in common, that the receptacles for the honey, in the case of bees, or of other food-materials, in the case of wasps, are fashioned very much as a potter fashions clay. The bee or wasp must collect the materials, and these must be appropriate materials, which connotes some discrimination, or selectivity. Then the materials must be manipulated, and the fact that a potter uses his hands while the bee or wasp uses its jaws is neither here nor there.

Many wasps build their nests of paper. In spring, in temperate regions, the queen wasp comes out of hibernation. All the worker wasps died the previous autumn and her task is to found a new colony. She flies to a wooden post or a log, or an old tree, and starts scraping fibres of wood from its surface with her jaws. She

(above)
Although most **bees** are not social, or colonial, the most commonly known ones are. These include the bumblebees, honeybees and stingless bees. Some build nests—which may be very big—in the branches of trees, others on the ground or elsewhere. The nests of ants, termites or even birds may also be occupied by bees.

(below)
Mud wasps use mud in much the same way that other wasps use the paper they make from wood, employing their saliva as a cement and adding the materials layer by layer. The growth lines on the nest are often clearly marked. This **mud wasp nest** lies underground, in a swamp. The nest of the **organ-pipe mud wasp** is a long hanging cylinder, and several of these together do indeed look like organ pipes. The nest is solely to house the eggs and larvae. It is not a home.

Leaf-cutter ants cut pieces out of leaves and take them back to their nests, where they are used as a compost for growing a fungus on which the ants feed. Some of their nests are enormous—one was said to have been twelve yards across! Not surprisingly, they can cause havoc in plantations.

(above)
The **paper nest** built by many wasps is like a bag with several layers of paper. Inside it are cells, also made of paper, which are arranged in rows or tiers. Wasps live in societies, each of which is composed of a single queen and her offspring.

(right)
Ant lions are the larvae of insects which look something like small dragonflies. They dig funnel-shaped pits in the sand and wait for insects to fall in. When they do, the ant lions seize them in their jaws.

converts this to paper by chewing it. First she lays a foundation of paper on the ceiling of a cavity in a tree, or wherever the nest is to be built. From this she builds down, adding more and more paper as required, making innumerable journeys to collect it. When the foundations are complete, she makes half-a-dozen cells in which she lays her eggs, one to a cell. Workers hatch from these, and after they have been fed through the grub stage by the queen and have changed into the adult workers, they take over. The queen then merely lays more and more eggs.

When a colony of wasps is in fully working order there are thousands of workers to gather wood, convert it to paper and lay the paper in place to enlarge the outer covering of the nest, or to increase the number of cells in which the queen will lay her eggs. In effect, we have something of the same situation as we have in the Venus' flower-basket, in that the worker wasps are all independent, yet co-operating to produce a pattern or design. The different species of paper-using wasps each build a nest to a definite pattern, so that an expert looking at the nest can quickly tell the species of wasp that built it. The worker wasps are doing no more, and no less, than the cells of the Venus' flower-basket: working autonomously yet co-operating in a fixed plan. And there is no more intelligence in the work of bees or wasps other than is implied in a selectivity and manipulative skill subordinated to an inherited pattern of behavior.

However, this is not to say that the process is wholly automatic,

After digging a tunnel or finding one of the right length and bore, the female **leaf-cutting bee** builds a number of separate nests, which look a lot like cigar stubs. These nests are made from pieces of leaves cut by the bee and flown back to the tunnel. Using her jaws as scissors, she cuts each piece to size, so that every cutting will fit exactly into position and overlap those next to it. The nests themselves lie end to end, from the blind end of the tunnel almost to its entrance, and each is filled with a mixture of pollen and honey and has one egg laid in it.

for if the nest of a wasp colony is damaged the wasps will repair it, just as a living Venus' flower-basket will repair a rent in its skeleton, or, for that matter, a mollusk will repair a broken shell. This ability to recognize damage and to repair it is perhaps more remarkable than any other feature of animal building. It is a skill possessed even by plants!

To return to the actual building construction we may consider the pattern of the leaf-cutting bee. The female bee, once she has mated, starts building. First, she needs a tunnel of the correct length and bore. She may excavate this herself, in a post or in the trunk of a tree. It needs to be about five to six inches long and a little over a quarter of an inch in diameter, although these dimensions will vary somewhat with the species. Should the bee find a tunnel already made she will use it instead of making a fresh one. It has been known for a leaf-cutter bee to use a tunnel already made in the ground by some other insect, provided it is of the right proportions.

It is easy to speak glibly of "blind instinct", but when a leaf-cutter bee chooses a tunnel already made, instead of digging a fresh one, she does something which in a human being would be called showing common sense. At least, there is a measure of adaptability difficult to separate from intelligence. There is seeming intelligence also in the way the nest is constructed, although this must largely follow an inherited pattern of activity.

Within the tunnel the leaf-cutting bee makes a number of separate nests lying one behind the other, each filled with a mixture of pollen and honey, and in each she lays one egg. These nests, usually described as thimble-shaped but looking more like cigar stubs, lie end to end, from the blind end of the tunnel almost to its entrance. To make a nest the bee cuts pieces out of leaves, using her jaws as scissors, and flies with each piece back to the tunnel to place it in position. She has to cut a circle for each end of the nest, and each of the several pieces making up the sides must be shaped according to the position it will occupy; so each piece must have the correct curves, and must be of such a size as to overlap its neighbors. When lightly cemented together the whole must be leak-proof, able to hold the semi-fluid contents. However, we may be sure that a leaf-cutting bee does not have to think out the shape of each piece as she goes to cut it. Totally blind instinct is at work, but it is nonetheless remarkable for all that.

Throughout animal architecture there is this combination of mainly inherited pattern of behavior joined with some ability to adapt or change according to circumstances. The ability to adapt is sometimes spoken of as plastic behavior, when the animal possessing it is too low in the scale to justify the use of the word "intelligence". But clearly, the distinction between these two qualities must sometimes be difficult to draw.

Instinct or Intelligence?

THERE IS A TYPE OF INSECT known as caddis flies. Their larvae live at the bottoms of ponds and streams. The larvae have long soft bodies and have been called caddis worms as a consequence.

The original diving bell is built by the **water spider**. It makes a thimble-shaped bell of silk and attaches it by silk strands to the submerged parts of water plants, with the mouth of the bell directed downwards. This bell is then filled with air. To do this the spider goes to the surface, pushes the top of its abdomen into the air, traps a bubble of air among the hairs on its abdomen, swims down to the bell and releases the air inside it. The spider lives inside the bell and lays its eggs there.

(right)
At the bottom of ponds and streams live the **caddis fly larvae,** carrying their "homes" about with them. To protect their soft bodies these larvae build a tube, using whatever small materials they can find. It seems that this tube must be as long as their naked bodies, but once they are covered as far as their heads, their impulse to build ceases.

(right)
To protect its eggs from too much water or too little, the **Brazilian tree-frog** builds a mud "nest" about a foot across and three or four inches deep. This miniature pool holds the eggs and a small amount of water.

(below)
All spiders produce silk. Some merely lay a trail of it as they move along the ground, but others spin a beautiful **geometric web** as a snare to catch insects. As the spider grows bigger, the amount of silk it can spin increases and it enlarges its web. Whether or not this behavior is wholly due to instinct is an unsettled question.

Having soft bodies, and being otherwise without protection, the caddis worm defends itself by building a tube in which it shelters. The tube may be made of grains of sand, particles of leaves or twigs, or any small materials that lie to hand on the bottom. The caddis worm has a pair of hooks on the hind end of the body, which it fastens into the rear walls of the tube, so that when the front part of the body, bearing the legs, is pushed out and the caddis worm starts to walk it carries its tube with it. Clearly, the most efficient tube is one of just the right length to permit the caddis worm to walk about with only a small part of the front portion of the body exposed, at the same time keeping its hooks in the rear end of the tube to enable it to withdraw rapidly into the tube when danger threatens.

A caddis worm has to make no decisions in building the tube to the correct length. It has the impulse to add fresh materials to the tube, but experiment has shown that as soon as the tube reaches to just behind its head that impulse dies down. Moreover, a caddis worm shows little selectivity in the materials it uses: it takes whatever is to hand, which is in striking contrast to the way the single-celled animals will pick out exactly the same sizes or shapes from among a miscellaneous assortment. No more telling indication could be found to show how little architectural achievements in animals are dependent on the development of the nervous system. A caddis worm has a well-developed nervous system and something of a brain yet shows less discrimination than a single-celled animal with neither of these.

Spiders that spin the orb-webs incite strongly conflicting views. The layman is apt to contemplate their beautifully geometric webs and marvel at the skill and also the intelligence of spiders. The scientist who studies spiders is inclined to the opposite view. He sees this as a prime example of instinctive working because, as a writer on the subject once put it, all spiders of the same species spin to the same pattern, they spin the same pattern of web the first time they build, they never alter the pattern no matter how many webs they build, and no matter how many webs they build in the course of a lifetime they never improve on them. It is, however, an over-simplification, even while it is broadly correct. The pattern of the web differs slightly with age, with sex, and it also differs in small details from one individual to another, even within a single species.

But if we are to accept, as is reasonable, that the work of an orb-spider is a first-class example of instinctive behavior, we have also to accept it as showing that instinct is not so blind after all. The web may be spun and re-spun to a more or less rigid pattern time after time, but there are two important features to be kept in mind.

To start at the beginning, the female garden spider, which spins an orb-web, lays her eggs in a silken cocoon. When the spiderlings first hatch they keep together, in the vicinity of the cocoon. After a few days they disperse, and each starts its own web. The first web the spiderling spins is small, and in its pattern it is only a shadow of the web the adult spider spins, in that there are only a few radial threads and a few spiral threads. The next web it spins is not much better but within a few days the true pattern begins to emerge.

It is not wholly unreasonable to view the young spider's web-spinning as an "emergent skill". This is a phrase that has been used about children and it could well be adopted, at least tentatively, for animals. A boy with a pocket-knife starts by whittling wood and in a short while finds himself carving the wood into recognizable shape. The whittling is, in a sense, instinctive, certainly it is intuitive, and the wood-carving it leads to is untaught. It seems to be much the same with the spiderling: the impulse to spin a web is innate but the performance appears to be imperfect at first. There is, however, one

Among the reeds and cattails of salt and freshwater marshes of North America, the **long-billed marsh wren** builds its large, bulky nest, domed at the top and with a side entrance. This is the work of the male, in whom the urge to build is so strong that he builds several nests, only one of which is used. The female merely lines the nest that she has chosen.

important difference between the child and the spider: the child's wood-carving can be vastly improved in time, either from experience or from tuition received, usually from both. This cannot be said of a spider's web-spinning.

It may be that an emergent skill has something in common with plastic behavior, in being based on an innate pattern yet leaving a margin for adaptive activities. In spiders plastic behavior is seen in the way a spider deals with its web as it grows older. As a spider increases in size so the amount of silk it can spin increases, as does the size of its web. A larger web requires a larger framework, and we find, for example, that a spider building on a window frame will, as the days pass, move outwards and sling its web from the brickwork, to give it a greater expanse. Even when spinning its web among foliage this same adjustment must often be made, because leaves and twigs are not static. The main alteration in a spider's web-spinning is, however, in the size of the frame it spins, and to understand this we need to follow the structures it makes, step by step, up to the completion of the web. In doing so, also, we can understand more clearly how mechanistic is the pattern of behavior that results in the completed web.

The first part of the frame laid down is a horizontal thread known as the bridge. From each end of this a thread is carried down, so that either a triangle is formed, or a fourth thread is added to form a square. Sometimes the frame is more elaborate and forms a polygon, usually pentagonal or hexagonal. Within this frame a number of radii are constructed which do not quite meet in the middle, so that a hole is left bounded by a circle of silk, known as the hub. Starting from the hub a spiral of non-sticky silk is laid down. When this is completed the spider has a scaffolding over which it can travel to lay down the sticky, or viscid, thread, the essential part of the web, since a web is primarily a snare for flying insects. The non-sticky thread is temporary and is normally removed as the spider goes round laying down the viscid thread.

It is not possible here to treat the mechanics of web-building in detail, but a few observations will suffice to show the general principles. Once the frame is completed the spider lays down the first radius, from the hub to the frame. This completed, it walks four steps along

(left)
If approached, a **sand crab** will try to return to its burrow, but if its escape is blocked it will race across the sand with astonishing speed. Sand crabs live in air-filled igloos. They are also called ghost crabs, for on dimly-lighted nights they look pale and ghostly.

(center)
Where moles are numerous, the ground beneath the surface becomes a labyrinth of **mole tunnels.** Using its front feet as a combination of pick and shovel, a mole tunnels through the ground. Then it turns around and pushes the loose earth out to the surface with its snout.

(right)
Prairie dogs were once found in colonies numbering hundreds of millions on the prairies of the midwestern United States. Since these rodents dig burrows in the ground, the burrowed areas, or towns, of such colonies can be enormous. One town in 1901 was estimated to cover 100 by 240 miles and to contain 400 million prairie dogs.

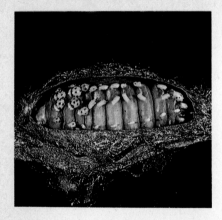

The caterpillars of many moths spin silken threads which are woven into a **cocoon** as the caterpillar turns round and round. This is a marvelous protection, for the cocoon is not only waterproof but, because of the air trapped between the fibers, it also provides a constant temperature for the chrysalis which the caterpillar becomes. However, that will not be of much help to the caterpillar shown here, since it is already heavily parasitized with the grubs of the ichneumon wasp.

Among spiders, the best performance is surely that of the **trapdoor spider** of the tropics. After making a silk-lined tunnel in the ground with a thickened rim at the entrance, this spider constructs a hinged lid that fits the opening exactly. The spider comes out of its tunnel to catch insects and withdraws when in danger, and as it goes in and out it opens and closes its trapdoor. One might almost say it had some understanding of mechanical devices.

the frame to start the next radius. Because it does this each time the radii are all more or less equidistant from each other, and the angles they make with each other at the hub are more or less equal.

When laying down the spiral threads the spider starts with the end of one foreleg touching the hub and its body along a radius; the silk is given out by the group of spinnerets at the tip of the abdomen. So as the spider travels round the radii its forelegs and the length of its body in combination furnish, so to speak, a measuring rod, keeping the threads of the spiral equidistant. A gardener, marking out a flower bed by rule-of-thumb methods, would do much the same but using his feet. The essential difference is that the gardener thinks things out: the spider works from what is called instinct.

Naturally, the question has arisen whether a spider uses any intelligence at all in fabricating this snare. Tests have been made, and a few of the results are given here. A portion of spiral thread in one sector (that is between two radii) was removed while the spider was in process of laying down the non-viscid spiral. When the spider came round again to this point it made no attempt to replace the missing thread but hitched the silk onto the spiral next to the missing part. That means its foreleg touched only thin air where a silk thread should have been so it reached out until it touched silk, and fastened the thread there.

Spiders use touch more than any other sense, so it must remain a matter of opinion whether this is an unfair test, or whether the spider was making the best of a bad job, or whether it is unable to deviate from a fixed pattern of behavior.

Other tests have been no more conclusive. They include moving spiders from the webs they are spinning and putting them on webs at a more advanced stage than those they were working on. Out of twenty-eight spiders treated in this manner sixteen remained motionless or else destroyed the web. Seven went on spinning as if nothing had happened, so duplicating work already done. Five continued the work from the stage at which they found the web.

We could interpret the actions of the sixteen as the result of a frustration. The next seven continued mechanically the actions they were engaged upon. And the five showed an ability to adapt their behavior to changed circumstances. One wonders how twenty-eight human beings rudely and brusquely interrupted when engaged on an essential task would have responded. Probably in much the same ways!

Another set of tests consisted of putting spiders that had never spun a web before onto partly spun webs, the rightful owners having been removed. Not surprisingly, most of them failed to do anything purposeful, but a few actually completed the web. That these few should have gone on to complete the webs is, to say the least, quite remarkable.

These are but a small sample of the experiments made to test the motivations of spiders. The first thing they show is that it is extremely difficult to come to any firm conclusion. The results of the tests vary with the experimenter, and the interpretations tend to vary more still. In summing them up it seems fair to say that spiders spin webs on a plan that varies according to the species, that the work itself is largely instinctive, using the word in a broad context, but that there are indications of an ability to adapt the behavior to circumstances and that this ability varies with the individual.

This summary is applicable in a general way to all animals, with the amount of adaptability shown becoming greater as we ascend the animal scale and as the nervous system becomes more highly developed. This makes it nevertheless remarkable that such superb results should be achieved at all levels of animal organization.

Understanding Mechanical Devices

Not all spiders spin webs, although all use silk in some way, if only to make a cocoon to shelter their eggs, but the best performance is probably that of the trapdoor spider of the tropics. This not only excavates a vertical tunnel in the ground and lines it with silk, it makes a thickened rim at the entrance to the tunnel and constructs on this a hinged circular lid that fits the entrance exactly. Moreover, the trapdoor spider opens and closes the trapdoor in a highly skilful fashion, as if it had an appreciation of mechanical devices.

This last phrase is used here deliberately because it is a feature of so many animals, especially, but not exclusively, of mammals. Even those that make no attempt to build, or are incapable of constructing even a simple shelter, seem endowed with a capacity for understanding mechanical devices. This comes out especially in the way rats will sometimes find ways of escaping from traps, and in the way squirrels will open boxes and other receptacles to take food contained in them. It is seen also in the stories of dogs, horses and others opening gates and doors. Some birds have been known to perform similar feats, and while in these and other instances there is the possibility of their

(below)
The **termitaria** shown here, each the home of a colony of termites, are taller than a man. They could be called skyscrapers if we consider the size of the animals that built them. Sometimes incorrectly termed "white ants," termites are really close relatives of cockroaches. Their social organization is extremely complex, including queens and their mates, sometimes different kinds of workers and several types of soldiers who protect the workers. All termites live in colonies, but not all build termitaria.

(left)
When the tide is out, the **Malayan soldier crab** comes out of its igloo to feed, scooping sand into its mouth, sifting out the edible part and casting away the remaining sand as a pellet. As the returning tide approaches, the crab begins to dig, making building pellets of sand with which it constructs an igloo around itself with a bubble of air enclosed in it. After the water covers the igloo, the crab can remain inside until the tide moves out once again.

having learned accidentally how to do these things, there is a significant number of examples which cannot be dismissed so readily.

Whether the trapdoor spider's actions in opening and closing its trapdoor come within this range is doubtful, but in view of some of the surprises modern research has revealed it is unwise to be dogmatic. Nevertheless, assessing these actions at their lowest, as a purely innate pattern of behavior, it has to be admitted that a high degree of manipulative skill is involved, as it is also in the behavior of the Malayan soldier crab. This species also provides a contrast in two skills, one useless and the other highly functional. The crab receives its name because as the tide recedes and uncovers the sandy shores soldier crabs, small and long-legged, come out in their thousands, often moving about in serried ranks, like a rag-tag army. While the tide is out they feed by scooping sand into their mouths with their claws. The mouth-parts are in constant motion, sifting the edible matter from the sand, which is then ejected as a pellet. The crab brushes this aside with its claw, so that the shore becomes littered with these tiny pellets.

There are many related species of these sand-sifting crabs. Some stay near the entrances to their burrows to feed and the pellets of sand they reject become arranged in geometric patterns, each species having a characteristic pattern. There is certainly no question of deliberate design here, even though a pattern is produced. The pattern merely reflects the way in which a particular species of crab feeds.

As the tide flows and the water's edge begins to approach one of the Malayan soldier crabs it begins to dig into the sand and push pellets upwards. These have nothing to do with feeding. They are building pellets. Rapidly, the soldier crab pivots throwing up a circle of pellets to form a rampart. Further pellets are added, one by one, as the crab digs, pushes up and moves around to dig and push up once more, until a dome of pellets, with a hole in the top, is formed over it. This hole is plugged with a final pellet.

Very soon after the final pellet is placed in position the water covers the sandy igloo. Inside, the crab digs deeper, all the time pushing the sand upwards, so that the bubble of air enclosed in the dome of pellets sinks deeper into the sand, for the crab to breathe until the ebbing tide brings it out once again to feed.

Here, then, are two innate patterns of behavior. One has a useless end-result but is the consequence of a purposeful feeding action. The other has a direct purpose, to enclose a bubble of air for breathing.

The Complex Termitarium

Perhaps the most remarkable building structure in the whole animal kingdom is the termitarium, the home of a colony of termites, sometimes miscalled white ants. They are, in fact, no rela-

(opposite page, top left and right) While some termites make long tunnels underground, others build huge mounds on the surface like these, which may be as high as 20 feet or—in one case—as broad as 100 yards. These **termitaria** are made of mud cemented with saliva, and once hardened they are extremely strong. Inside the mounds are chambers and galleries which provide ventilation and through which the inhabitants can wander freely. There is a central chamber in which the huge queen spends her time laying eggs, and in other chambers fungi are grown that reduce the wood on which the termites feed to a more digestible form. It is notable that this amazing building achievement is only possible when there are great numbers of these insects, because individually they are helpless.

(left)
Carpenter ants build their nests in dead or decaying wood, making tunnels and laying their eggs in them. When an occupied log is split open, the ants quickly move the eggs and undeveloped insects to a safer area.

tives of true ants but are among the more primitive of insects, close relatives of cockroaches. Not all species of termites build termitaria, but all live in highly-organized colonies.

A colony of true ants contains three kinds of individuals: a queen, the males and the workers. It is much the same for bees and wasps. The queen founds the colony and then devotes her life to laying eggs. The real work of the ant-hill, hive or wasp-nest is carried on by the workers, which are sterile females. Termites have a more complex organization, with a subsidiary caste of queens and males, sometimes several kinds of workers, and also several castes of soldiers for protecting the workers.

Some termites build underground, driving tunnels horizontal with the surface, which may be up to 200 yards long. Other species construct huge mounds on the surface, of mud cemented with saliva which, once it has hardened, needs a pick-axe to break it. Some of these mounds are twenty feet high. One termitarium, in Africa, is 100 yards across, and a village has been built on top of it, which only goes to show how strong it is.

After digging a cavity in the sea-bed for her eggs, the female **octopus** builds a wall around it with large pebbles and stones. In moving these stones she reaches out with one of her arms and covers the stone, then passes it from sucker to sucker along the undersurface of her arm. The octopus also collects rocks and uses them to plug the entrance of its den. It is one of the most highly developed and intelligent of all invertebrates, which are animals that lack backbones.

A termitarium of this sort has a central chamber in which the enormously large queen spends her time laying eggs, attended by a band of workers. There are other chambers in which fungi are cultured that reduce the wood, on which the termites feed, to a more digestible form. And throughout, this vast mound is a succession of chambers and of galleries through which the inhabitants can wander freely. One feature of a termitarium, which has only become appreciated within recent years, is that the architecture of the galleries includes an air-conditioning system. That is, the ventilation is so arranged that the interior of the colony is kept at a constant temperature and humidity.

It is more interesting still that this should be the work of insects each of which, as an individual, is mentally so ill-equipped as to merit no other word than stupid. One termite on its own has been shown experimentally to be quite helpless. A few together, isolated from the rest of the colony, are little better. Put a few more together and they will start to use mud for building but can still achieve little. When, however, they are present in large numbers they combine to produce, like the cells of the Venus' flower-basket, a marvel of engineering construction.

The galleries are constructed as a series of pillars to which vaulted roofs are added. One small feature of this work is sufficient to illustrate, but without explaining, how the termites' co-operation works. They construct pillars by adding pellets in layers, placed like bricks, in the usual manner of constructing pillars. When the requisite height is reached one termite begins to build a line of pellets horizontally from the top of the pillar. Meanwhile, from an adjacent pillar another termite builds outwards to meet the first. Left alone, the two horizontal lines of pellets meet perfectly in the middle. Take one of the termites away, experimentally, and the other termite will stop building at the point where its horizontal line of pellets should have met the other to complete the arch.

The fact that the two lines of pellets should meet accurately in the middle is remarkable enough. The fact that in some species the worker termites doing the work are blind makes it even more remarkable.

If we are to judge from a recent account of the behavior of a female octopus, there is much yet to be learned about the building activities of other of the lower animals. John Woods has recently described watching octopuses off the island of Capri, in the Mediterranean, in the course of skin-diving. The female octopus excavates a cavity among the sand, pebbles and rocks on the sea-bed in which to lay her eggs. She builds a wall around the cavity and then stations herself on it to repel intruders. The really interesting part concerns the means she uses to move the large pebbles and stones to make the wall. She stretches one of her arms until the tip covers the stone to be moved, then this stone is passed from sucker to sucker along the

Flying squirrels glide from tree to tree; they do not really fly. North American species usually take over deserted holes of woodpeckers and line them with shredded bark and dry leaves and then make an inner lining of soft materials such as moss, feathers and fur. Occasionally they make an outside nest of sticks and line it in the same way.

A great burrower, the **badger** often digs a complicated system of connecting tunnels. It keeps its home very clean and has periodic spring-cleaning sessions during which it throws out its old bedding.

Although the **bald eagle** is the national emblem of the United States, it has not been safe from the hunter's gun. Today it is common only in parts of Alaska. Eagles usually build very large nests made of twigs and sticks in a tree or on a cliff.

undersurface of the arm. Stones as much as two pounds in weight were transported or lifted vertically by this method.

Beside the achievements of the invertebrates considered up to this point, even the most outstanding birds' nests represent a relatively low standard of architecture, despite the higher development of the bird's brain. In fact, as already said, the most striking feature of animal architecture seems to be that it has little correlation with the degree of development of the brain and central nervous system.

Animals are divided into invertebrates, or animals without backbones, and vertebrates, or animals with backbones. The first are often called the lower animals, the second constitute the higher animals. The

invertebrates either have no recognizable brain or nervous system, or, where there is a brain and central nervous system, both are decidedly inferior to those of vertebrates. Yet for all that, as we have seen, in virtually all classes of invertebrates there are species showing remarkable building skills.

The Building Skills of Vertebrates

AMONG VERTEBRATES we naturally turn to birds for examples of manipulative skills, because nest-building is more common among birds than in other classes of vertebrates. Yet even among other

In the late autumn when the salmon spawn and then die, these eagles gather to feed on the dead fishes. Other scavengers, such as gulls, magpies and bears, also join in the feast. Coming in for a landing here is a young **bald eagle,** which lacks the white head characteristic of the adult bird.

vertebrates than birds, as among invertebrates, we find building skills in all classes, from the lowest to the highest, and some are quite unexpected.

The lowest of the vertebrates are the lampreys, at one time included among fishes but now placed on their own as a more primitive group. A lamprey is eel-like and has a large funnel-shaped sucker at the front end of the body, surrounding the mouth. It feeds by fastening onto the body of a fish with this sucker and rasping away its flesh with a filelike tongue.

Some lampreys live in the sea but come up the rivers to spawn. Before spawning male and female combine to make a pit into which the eggs will be laid. With their suckers they lift pebbles and carry them away until a pit six inches deep and two to three feet in diameter is prepared.

A lamprey has a brain, of very simple structure, which acts more as a control of the muscles and to receive sensory perceptions than for working out problems. It is the more remarkable that it should behave some-

(below)
Lampreys, the lowest vertebrates, are more primitive than fish. They are eel-like and have a large, funnel-shaped sucker around their mouths. This sucker is used for fastening themselves onto the bodies of fish on which they feed.

(right)
Sea lampreys move up the rivers at breeding time, the males going first, followed later by the females. They select a suitable depression in a sandy bed and remove any stones that may be in the way, placing them along the sides of the pit as a sort of protective wall. After the eggs have been laid and fertilized, both parents cover them with sand and stones. The adults then leave and die.

what after the manner of the slaves building the pyramids. Its nest-building must be seen therefore as due to an innate pattern of behavior. Nevertheless, the result of it is a neat piece of building construction, the lamprey using the only organ it has, the sucker, that is capable of being employed for purposes of manipulation.

The great majority of fishes lay their eggs at random in the sea or in fresh water, and having done so take no further interest in them. Among freshwater fishes, and some shore fishes, however, there is often a degree of parental care. This may range from incubating the eggs in a pouch on the abdomen of the male, as in sea-horses, to holding the eggs in the mouth, as in those tropical fishes known as mouth-breeders, or to building some form of nest. In salmon the female digs a shallow depression in the sand on the bed of a river, using her own body, with wriggling movements, as the excavating tool. Some birds do little more than this when building a nest. There are freshwater fishes that blow bubbles to form a raft for the reception of the eggs, and there are others

(below)
Although building achievements of fishes are not very impressive, there are a few exceptions. The best example is the nest-building of **sticklebacks.** The three-spined species builds on the bottom and the ten-spined species off the bottom, among reed stems.

(left)
The male stickleback constructs a **nest of water-reeds** glued together with threads secreted from his kidneys. When the structure is finished, he tries to lure as many females as possible to lay their eggs in it. After the young hatch, the male remains on guard.

that use a crude chamber among the larger pebbles on the river-bed. The miller's thumb or bullhead is a good example. The male excavates a trough in the sand under a large pebble for this purpose.

The best example of nest-building among fishes is found in the sticklebacks. It is the male stickleback that builds the somewhat crude nest, of pieces of water plants glued together with gelatinous threads secreted from his kidneys, which change function at this time.

Considering there are about thirty thousand different kinds of fishes, their achievements as builders are very low, and the sample given here represents the most they can do. Nevertheless, in view of the way fishes are built and in view of their requirements for living and breeding it is remarkable that even a few of them should show talents in this direction, especially when we remember that frogs and toads, as well as most reptiles, which have the advantage of legs and toes, do very little better. One result of having legs is that burrowing is much easier. However, many invertebrates other than insects that lack legs also burrow, and so do some fishes, usually in soft mud, although there are fishes capable of digging quite deep pits by blowing water at the sand.

Apart from burrowing, few amphibians or reptiles show any constructive or manipulative capacities. Such as there are, however, support the idea that in all animals some architectural potentiality is present even if it is not used, or is used to only a slight extent. For example, an Argentinian frog makes a foam nest for its eggs. As the female lays them she also gives out a certain amount of mucus. This the male, while still clinging to the female's back, paddles rapidly with his hind-legs, beating the mucus into a foam which lies among the vegetation in marshes like snow. A closely-related species makes an underground burrow but also creates a foam, inside the burrow.

Some tree-frogs, in Africa and Asia, construct foam nests among leaves, and the leaf-frogs of Central and South America make nests of leaves, using the stickiness of the eggs to gum the leaves together. The Brazilian tree-frog, known as the smith frog because its voice sounds like the clanging of a blacksmith's hammer, constructs a pond within a pond for its eggs. This consists of a circular dyke of mud in shallow water near the bank, thrown up by the frog, giving a pool about six inches deep and a foot or more across, with the rim of the pool just above water level. The inner surface of the dyke is carefully smoothed down with the forelegs.

Reptiles, except for burrowing species, do little more than the amphibians. A snake living in the United States constructs a bottle-shaped underground chamber, with a vertical shaft to the surface, in which eggs are laid. The king cobra makes a nest of dead leaves, bending the front part of its body into a loop to rake the leaves together. Finally, some crocodiles make nests of rotting vegetation over their eggs, to form an incubator, the female staying near at hand to guard the nest.

It is in birds more especially that building talents are most evident,

(opposite page)
Most familiar to us are the building talents of birds. The **bearded tit** or reedling constructs a nest that is shaped like a flask or bottle. It lives among reeds, feeding on insects and seeds.

(above)
Birds have only a beak and hind-feet to work with, since their wings take the place of forelegs. Yet they construct some remarkable homes. Among the simpler achievements are the **cup-shaped mud nests** of flamingos.

(above, right)
The **house martin** makes its nest with pellets of mud and lines the inside with a soft covering.

which is remarkable since their forelegs have been modified to wings and they have only the beak and the hind-feet to use. Apart from cuckoos and other parasitic birds, such as cow-birds, that use the nests made by other species in which to lay their eggs, there are quite a few species that make no nest at all. Nightjars merely lay their eggs on the ground. Owls use a hollow tree or a nest abandoned by another species.

Many birds merely scrape a shallow depression in the surface of the ground, at most adding a little dried grass. But most birds do better than this. Their nests may range from the cup-shaped mud nests of flamingos to the elaborate nests of song-birds. The usual technique is to lay a foundation of nesting materials and, as the sides of the cup begin to grow, the bird pivots on this to give the cup-shape. At the same time the materials are built into the walls by skilful use of the beak.

A Variety of Nests

THE TYPE AND FORM of birds' nests afford a wide diversity, and two aspects only need special mention here. One is an examination of how far learning plays a part. The other is the consideration of some of the more remarkable nests.

In many species there seems to be no learning at all. Young birds taken from the nest and reared in isolation experimentally build nests exactly as their parents did. Yet they had no opportunity of learning how it was done, or of imitating the actions of other individuals of their species. In these, there seems to be little doubt that the whole of their skill is innate. Other birds, by contrast, have the general idea of how to build but improve with practice. The male rook, for example, which does all the building, shows in his first year increasing skill in handling the sticks, used for making the nest, as the nest-structure increases in size. Moreover, watching the same individual rook in its second year, we see that the nest is built faster this second time, the bird making fewer

mistakes and, altogether, working as if he were more experienced and had remembered the lessons of the previous year.

These remarks doubtless apply to some other species of birds also: the rook is specially named here because its progress has been studied. In the rook, also, it is noticeable that the bird does not put the sticks into the nest haphazardly. He may push a stick in at one place, stand back as if surveying the results of his handiwork, then come forward, remove the stick and push it in elsewhere. Such actions as these are difficult to interpret, except to suppose that judgment of some kind is being exercised.

For the extreme examples of superlative nest-building we need to go to birds such as weavers, orpendolas and tailor-birds. On the way we can admire the tiny cups built by hummingbirds of plant materials held together by spider's silk, or the excavating abilities of sand martins and kingfishers that dig tunnels running into sandy banks as much as three feet. There are also the house martins making their nests of pellets of mud, and the oven-bird of South America that makes a massive mud house with an entrance hall leading to the nesting-chamber.

Some birds sling their nests hammock-fashion between the stems of tall plants, but the oropendolas weave sleevelike tubes of dry grass two or three feet long, suspended from branches of trees. Some people regard these as the acme in bird architecture. Many birds of the weaver family make similar nests, but in this family the peak is reached by the social weavers with their "tenement-blocks". One of these apartment dwellings in a tree may be as much as ten feet high and fifteen feet in diameter, built by as many as three hundred pairs of birds. It is a conglomeration of individual nests, all joined and sharing a common roof which may have a straw thatch.

For an exquisite performance the tailor-birds of South-east Asia are hard to beat. The nest proper is not a tidy structure, but it is enclosed within two large leaves that are sewn together at the edges. To sew

(above, left)
A **white stork's nest** may be built with reeds, grasses, branches and lumps of earth as well as rags or paper. When returning from their winter migration homes, storks will go to their old nests and rebuild them. After a number of years these rebuilt nests can become extremely large.

(above)
Once the foundation for its nest is laid, the bird builds up the sides of the cup, skillfully weaving the materials into the wall with its beak. The **golden oriole** constructs its nest in the fork of two horizontal branches, which makes the nest more secure.

In Africa it is not unusual to come upon large numbers of **weaver bird nests** hanging from the branches of a single tree. These nests are long, hanging pouches with a sleeve open at the bottom through which the bird enters or leaves.

them the bird first pierces a hole with its beak, threads a strip of dry grass through this, then knots the thread on the outside.

The finest architecture in the bird world is, however, not seen in a nest but in the bowers made by the bower-birds of Australia and New Guinea. A typical bower consists of a platform of sticks laid on the ground into which other sticks are planted vertically to form two parallel palisades enclosing an avenue. It is the work of the male, and he uses it as a stamping ground in which to display to the female. Moreover, he decorates the bower with bright objects, such as flowers, leaves, shells and feathers, and, in some species, he daubs the walls of the bower with juices of berries, even to fraying the end of a small stick to use as a paint-brush.

In decorating the bower almost any bright object may be used, but the various bower-birds tend to show preferences for certain hues. They

(top, left)
For their size, **weaver birds** build some of the largest nests. Some species that are only the size of sparrows construct nests as large as tents. Indeed, the social weavers live in huge apartment dwellings that are hung in a tree and that may be as much as ten feet high and fifteen feet in diameter.

(left)
This **oriole's nest** is hung in a yucca plant. Most species of orioles use long fibers in weaving their sacklike nests, sometimes creating hundreds of complicated loops and knots during the construction.

(right)
Weaver birds are experts at the craft of weaving and their nests display some of the finest **workmanship** to be found among bird architects.

(right)
Unless it is gathering mud to build its nest, the barn swallow is unlikely to land on the ground at all. The **barn swallow's nest** is frequently hung on the rafters of a shed, barn or similar building.

(below)
On top of a tree or high rock, near water, the **osprey** (or fish hawk) constructs its nest. It catches fishes with its claws and takes them back to its nest to eat them. Birds which make their nests of sticks seem to exercise some judgment in placing the sticks in position.

will remove, and bury under dead leaves, any objects tinted otherwise than to their choice, which have been placed on the bower by the human experimenter. It has been shown by careful tests that some other birds seem to have preferences as to hues, but it is especially marked in bower-birds.

To this same family, the bower-birds, which is related to the birds-of-paradise, belong the gardener birds, or maypole-builders. Around the base of a sapling the maypole-builder erects an edifice of sticks, which may be as much as nine feet high, forming a sort of house or gazebo. In front of the "house" a lawn is laid out, bounded by a "hedge" of sticks and decorated with flowers and leaves, which are regularly renewed as they wither.

Remarkable as their works are, in the bower-birds there is the same building to a pattern according to the species as we have found elsewhere in the animal kingdom. That is, this astounding architectural skill is innate. And yet it is difficult to avoid the view that these birds possess an artistic sense. This seems evident when we see a bower-bird place a flower or a feather in position, then stand back, survey it with head on one side, hop forward, pick it up, place it elsewhere, and once again stand and survey it, rather as a rook does with its sticks. There seems to be clear evidence in the bower-bird of choice (or selectivity) as well as discrimination and artistic judgment.

In spite of what has been said here earlier about the building skills of

Few performances of nest-building skill can compare with that of the Asian **tailor-bird**. While the nest itself is not particularly remarkable, it is enclosed between two large leaves that are sewn together at the edges by the bird. To accomplish this the tailor-bird uses a strip of dry grass or vegetable fiber which it threads through the holes it has made with its beak.

(right)
Mammals as a group have the most highly developed brains in the animal kingdom. It is surprising, therefore, that their building achievements are often more remarkable for their size than for their complexity or skill. The enormous **burrows of prairie dogs,** for example, which are called towns, may extend over many miles in all directions. Except for their extent, though, these towns are not especially noteworthy.

Although the **rabbit** has only weak front feet, it excavates enormous burrows by scraping away the earth with its front feet and pushing it backwards with its strong hind feet. A colony of rabbits may dig numerous tunnels in a bank, which is then known as a **warren.** Some larger warrens have been known to extend nearly a quarter of a mile.

the lower animals, it is in birds more especially that we find the most widespread use of these skills. It is as if some overpowering urge in them must find expression; and this idea seems reinforced by the behavior of the male wren. He may build as many as a dozen nests, after which his mate selects one, lines it, and lays her eggs in it. We may argue that this gives the hen an opportunity to choose the best of several, but since the male will sometimes go on building fresh nests after she has laid, his activities give the impression of building for building's sake.

The Skillful Beaver

FINALLY, WE COME to the mammals, the group of animals most nearly like ourselves. They have the best brains of the whole animal world. They have limbs with toes, many of them with grasping toes or fingers. And the result is disappointing in some respects. There is a great deal of burrowing, especially by rodents, and in some species the size of the burrows can reach spectacular proportions, in species such as prairie dogs, badgers and moles. There is also widespread nest-building. This is at least as common as with birds, and in some species of shrews and rodents, particularly tree squirrels, it reaches a high standard of achievement. But the best nest-building by any species of mammals is well below that of such birds as the weavers, orpendolas, tailor-birds and others like these. For architectural achievements comparable to that of bower-birds we have to go to the beaver.

Muskrats show some comparison with beavers, and they build somewhat on the same plan, although less extensively and less skilfully. This may be as well since it leaves the field clear, allowing us to concentrate on the beaver, about which there is a greater conflict of opinion than on other animal builders.

It may be as well to begin by considering what it is beavers do. Typically, a pair of beavers settling in a fresh locality will dam a river

so that the water overflows its banks and creates a beaver pond. At or near the middle of the pond the pair build a lodge, with a central living room just above the level of the surrounding water and two or more entrances into this chamber opening below water level. To dam the river a main dam is constructed downstream of the future site of the pond and one or more secondary dams downstream of that. Upstream of the site of the pond one or more small, secondary dams are built.

The dam is built of branches and logs cut from trees growing in the vicinity, which the beavers themselves fell and dismember, transporting the materials to the site. It is started on the two banks, materials being added until the two arms meet in mid-stream to complete the dam. Stones, small boulders and mud are used to consolidate the dam and make it watertight. The lodge is built of similar materials.

Should the dam spring a leak, or should flood-waters cause an overflow, the beavers will repair the dam or raise its height. In fact, they

Since most mammals are four-footed and usually have toes, many of them grasping toes or fingers, we might consider them to be best-equipped for building. By most standards, however, this is rarely the case. Nest-building, particularly by such rodents as the **tree squirrel** (top left), may reach a high level, but not comparable to that of such birds as weavers and tailor-birds. The **common badger** (top right) digs extensive tunnels with many entrances, but what is most unusual about the burrows is their cleanliness. Even the work of the world's best tunneler, the **mole** (above left and right), is only an elaborate underground "highway system."

spend their lives felling trees, transporting them and keeping their dams and lodges in good repair.

By all standards it is a remarkable achievement for a pair or even for a family, of beavers to construct a dam which may be several hundreds of yards long and as much as twelve feet high. The core of the question is whether the beavers' work is intelligent or instinctive, and it is on this that opinion is so divergent. The fact that beavers always build in much the same way suggests that their activities are governed by an inherited behavior pattern. That is, their actions are instinctive. Yet engineers who have examined the dams maintain that the way beavers build them is the only way they could be built to make them effective. So their work could be intelligent.

The repairing of a dam also looks like intelligent work but there was a family of beavers living in a small lake in New York that had been produced by an artificial barrier of stone and cement. This barrier was in perfect condition, yet the beavers spent the whole of a summer "repairing" it. This looks like a lack of reasoning power associated with "blind instinct".

Those who believe in beaver intelligence claim that a beaver always fells a tree so that it falls towards the water where it is to be used. On the other hand, observers state this is not always so. So we could go on, producing examples of their work that look like intelligent activity, and countering these by arguments suggesting that all their extraordinary engineering skill is due to no more than those factors which make up what we call instinct. Nevertheless, when the heat of argument has died down, there is still the fact that when all the trees in the vicinity of a beaver pond have been felled, and the beavers have to work farther afield, instead of dragging the logs overland they will dig a canal and float them to where they are required. The canal may be up to half-a-mile long. It is difficult to believe that some judgment, even some decision-taking, is not involved in this.

(below)
Fan worms inhabit crevices in coral and fashion tubes for themselves by cementing sand grains together. Unlike most mammals, the fan worm shows considerable skill in its construction. It picks up each sand grain with its lips, moistens it with saliva and places it in position as a bricklayer would a brick, thus building a kind of circular tower around itself.

(right)
The **muskrat** makes a pile of grasses and rushes in the middle of a pond or stream and builds its nest in it. Although the plan of its work somewhat resembles the beaver's, it is far less extensive or skillful.

(left)
When a pair of beavers settle in a new locality, they dam a river so that the water overflows its banks and creates a beaver pond. The main **beaver dam** is constructed downstream of the future pond and made of branches and logs plastered with mud and weighted with stones and small boulders. It may be hundreds of yards long and up to twelve feet high.

(above)
It is an open question whether the **beaver's activity** is wholly the result of instinct or if it also shows intelligence. One argument in favor of intelligence is the way a beaver transports logs from afar, digging a canal and floating them instead of dragging them overland.

It may be that the argument, whether any part of this work is intelligent or whether all of it is instinctive, is vain, and that we need to look at the beavers' work in the light of what we have seen lower in the animal scale. With those things in mind we could argue that the main framework of a beaver's skill is due to an inherited pattern of behavior. But if we can allow a plastic behavior in bees and wasps, even more should we expect to find either plastic behavior, adaptability, or the ability to modify the inherited pattern, in one of the higher animals. Finally, it is surely wrong to argue about the word "intelligent", because the one thing that stands out from the discussion throughout this book is that the ability to make things cannot be correlated with what we normally understand by intelligence. We need to think in terms of a manipulative skill that is not necessarily linked with the higher mental faculties.

If further support is needed for this last remark it can be found in the manlike apes, the chimpanzee, gorilla and orangutan. These have brains only slightly inferior in size to our own. They have grasping hands, they can even use their feet as hands, yet the most any of them does in the wild is to make each night a crude sleeping platform, by

Having dammed the river, the beaver pair build a lodge near the middle of their pond. Inside this structure is a central living room just above the water level with two or more entrances opening under the water. Both dam and lodge are made of the same materials, and the **beavers are constantly busy** felling trees, cutting up branches and logs, transporting the materials and keeping everything in good repair.

pulling in the surrounding branches, up in a tree, and bending them in to make a leafy bed.

Harvest mice can do better than this. They will weave a globular nest of grass blades, adroitly pulling the fibres through the wall of the nest, with their teeth, to weave. A North American wood rat will make a house of sticks, with several passages and compartments. The stick-nest rats of Australia build in much the same way, but they live in deserts, in exposed positions, and where winds threaten their homes they lay stones on top of them to keep the sticks in position. All these are rodents merely lacking the brain power and the grasping fingers of the great apes.

The important difference is that the rodents have not only a little manipulative skill but also the urge to build. One of the striking features of a beaver is the way it will use its front paws as hands, or will hold

objects such as large stones under its chin to carry them. Even manipulative skill like this, on its own, is not enough. It has to have, like bees,
wasps and termites, or better still, the cock wren, an overweening urge
to build. Perhaps this is why beavers are always busy. It may also explain why beavers in the artificial pond in New York were repairing a
dam that needed no repairing—they could not stay idle but had to go
through the motions of building.

The raccoon of North America is a splendid example of the exact
reverse of this. It is a highly intelligent and resourceful animal. The
toes on both front and hind paws are highly mobile. Watching a raccoon
the observer is struck by the use the animal makes of all four paws
for grasping, and by the use made of the front paws in picking up food.
It is even claimed that a raccoon will untie knots in string. Yet a raccoon
does not even weave a nest: it merely sleeps in a hollow tree.

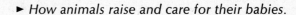
► *How animals raise and care for their babies.*

Animal Children

MOST NATURALISTS BELIEVE that there was a time, immeasurable ages ago, when life on the earth existed only in such primary form that we may think of it as scarcely more than a sort of seed or germ. This "primeval egg", which began the history of life on our planet, was what biologists call protoplasm—the basic life-substance, containing potentialities of growth and development; but in the beginning it would have provided no obvious hint of the great variety of living creatures that would eventually develop from it.

Over long ages, under countless influences of which many are still not fully understood, the life-substance developed and grew. It grew in complexity, becoming organized in variously shaping structures.

Naturalists, like poets, sometimes speak of the "tree of life". This is one way of saying that we can conceive the whole variety of living things as having a relationship with one another in much the same way as the branches and twigs of a tree are all related by their common origin in the seed from which the tree has grown. If we visualize such a "super family tree" then its branches and sub-branches will represent the various "families" of living things.

We can think of all the animal life in our world as a single great animal organization; this now vast, multiformed entity, comprising thousands of interrelated species functioning as a whole, was once only protoplasm. In this sense, all present living things shared in a common birth. The present diversity of animal forms has resulted from long ages of trial and error, and of slow changes, and adaptation to circumstances imposed by nature. By the time the first creatures that could be regarded as human came to appreciate the nature of the life with which they shared existence it was already richly differentiated; a

Like humans, many animals go through a childhood period in which they are given food, protection and special training by their parents. (top right) The baby swan, known as a **cygnet,** fears water and has to be taught to swim. (top, far right) The **honeyeater** produces a liquid food for its nestling and pumps it down its throat.

complex, teeming integration of inter-working parts. But while it is possible to speak of the story of animal life as a whole, it is also true that it is made up of the stories of separate species and of countless individual lives.

Every individual animal undergoes something like the growth-story naturalists believe they can trace in the common history of animal life. Every living creature around us has a birth, a youth, a growth toward its own kind of fulfillment and completion.

(below)
Gibbons, and most other primates, look remarkably human in the way they carry, hold and care for their young.

(above)
A mother **llama** takes care of her baby for the first few months of its life. Llamas are native to South America and related to camels. They were known to the ancient Incas and are still valued today for their ability to carry heavy loads in mountainous regions as well as for their wool, milk and flesh.

You and I start our existence as mere bits of life-stuff, mere seeds and eggs—as unlike a "person" as any particle of protoplasm when the world's life began. We reach our fulfillment able to "hold the whole world in our heads" by the developed technique of a complex process called thinking, able to perform acts requiring elaborate co-ordinations of muscle, nerve and mind. The ape called a gibbon starts its existence, like man, as only a fertilized egg. It reaches adulthood marked by such skills as being able to swing expertly from limb to limb among jungle trees and to make huge, well-judged leaps in order to catch birds in flight; it will know how to protect and raise its gibbon youngsters and how to quench its own thirst by dipping up a drink in its cupped hand.

The strikingly marked **zebras** are related to the type of horse we are all familiar with. Usually only one foal is born at a time, which can stand and run shortly after birth.

We Are Born with Only Two Traits of Character

WHEN A HUMAN BEING IS BORN into the world, an important part of its development is already in the past. The minute, fertilized egg which marks the beginning of a new individual life will have become, first, an embryo with few points of resemblance to the final complete creature it will come to be; gradually the embryo will have developed features and limbs, and the organs necessary for its further, future development outside the parental body. Not till then does birth normally occur; and even then, the new being is incomplete in the sense that its "personality" is a mere embryo of what it will eventually become. It consists of little more than a few well-defined instincts and reflexes. The newborn infant almost at once displays a natural understanding of using "distress signals" when it wants to be fed or comforted;

(right)
A female **stink bug,** or shield bug, lays her eggs on a leaf. She protects the eggs and larvae by covering them with her body until the young insects are able to fend for themselves. In this picture the **baby stink bugs** remain clustered around their birthplace. In general, insects do not require special care or training after they are born.

(below)
Young **bats** cling to their mother even in flight. Luckily they have a good grip, for the mother flies about, catching insects, with the young hanging on to the fur on her belly. When they become too large, they will be left in roosts, where the mother will visit and feed them.

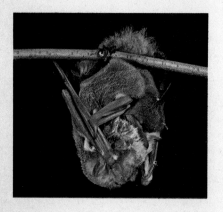

(below)
Clever and full of curiosity, a **young raccoon** is very active from the first day of its life. Its mother has to watch it all the time, as it likes to wander off climbing, exploring and digging. At night she takes her family on excursions and teaches them to fish with their paws and other important skills, which they learn by imitating her.

and it will instinctively grasp in its fist, very firmly, any suitable object, such as a finger, which touches its hand. Even the simple action of bringing the sight of both eyes to bear on a single object is a trick that has to be learned.

From that beginning, you and I have had to make the almost incredible change to becoming *people:* thinkers, doers, dealers with the adventure of human living. From a similar beginning, a baby gibbon has to make a change which is, for it, no less great. The ape will never develop powers of thought that equal our own; but it is no small thing to learn what foods to eat and what are the best ways to get them, to learn that snakes are dangerous and to learn how to judge whether a tendril will support one's weight *before* trusting oneself to it to swing from one tree to another. Looking at a baby gibbon, clutching its mother's shaggy body in helpless unknowing, who could guess it would grow to be such an accomplished ape?

Man shares with animals fundamental biological patterns, drives of impulse and emotion, sensory perceptions and experiences of many kinds throughout the cycle of life. There is plenty of evidence of our kinship with other creatures, and much of it is such as to stir in us at times a "fellow-feeling". Perhaps no other thing can make us feel more strongly the bond among all creatures than the way in which animals undergo the transitional adventures of childhood.

Let us take a look at what life's beginning and unfolding is like for some of these non-human infants. Childhood, in the human sense of the word, is a period of development in which the young animal enjoys parental affection, protection and special privileges. However, we need to understand that among many species this kind of fostering does not occur.

Some Animals Have No Childhood

THERE ARE PLENTY OF CREATURES whose manner of existence in adulthood makes anything resembling childhood in the human sense unnecessary. Such creatures come into the world already equipped with the powers they will need, in the form of instincts, automatic reflexes and guiding kinds of unconscious impulse operative from their birth and only very little modified by experience as life goes along.

Insects for instance, like worms and spiders, have a period of youth and undergo a process of growth; but they require no period of protection and training to help them develop "adult personalities", and they develop no special abilities other than those which they have on starting individual, independent life. Such creatures, even when very young, are never "infants" in any accepted sense of the word.

A moth or butterfly is never a baby. From the egg of a moth or butterfly there hatches a caterpillar, a creature so different that we can hardly think of it as the same being at all. The caterpillar, following a period of growing and moultings, is transformed into a pupa—a life form something like the caterpillar-that-was, something like the insect-to-come, but different from both. In the end, another transformation occurs, and the mature butterfly or moth comes into being, ready to generate a new cycle of lives. Nowhere in this system of reproduction and development is there anything that we could recognize as an equivalent of childhood.

Some Animals Are Never "Born"

AMONG THE VERY SMALL ANIMALS that naturalists call animalcules— tiny creatures such as the amoeba and paramecium, little organisms less than one one-hundredth of an inch long which teem in ponds, brooks and the sea—there is neither childhood nor the experience of

(bottom left)
A queen bee lays her **eggs in the hive,** one egg to a cell, where they develop through the **larva** and **pupa** stages to become perfectly-formed bees. When the **young bee** is ready to leave its cell, it is already an adult—without ever having had a childhood.

(bottom right)
The **silkworm** spins a **cocoon,** inside of which it develops into a **moth.** The fibers of this cocoon are used to make silk cloth. Neither caterpillars nor the moths and butterflies they become have true childhoods.

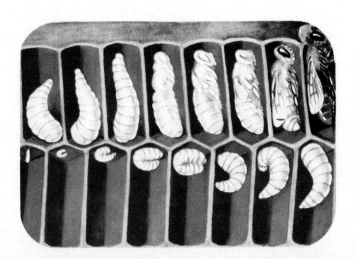

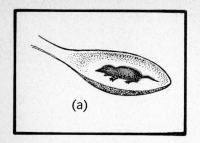

(a)

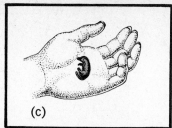

(c)

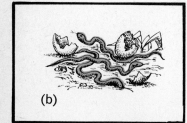

(b)

(d)

(left and bottom right)
The **comparative sizes of young animals** vary even more widely than the sizes of the adults. A newborn shrew (a) is shorter than a teaspoon, but even the adult is only two inches long. Baby snakes (b) may be a third the length of the parent. On the other hand, the kangaroo baby (c) will grow to be three thousand times heavier than its birth weight! Except for the bear (d), larger mammals such as the walrus (e) and elephant (f) give birth to well-developed young, which will increase only twenty to forty times in weight as they grow up.

(bottom left)
Although the **elk** calf is born with its eyes open and is able to walk within a few hours, it stays close to its mother for six months to a year.

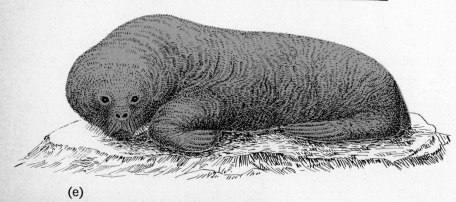

(e)

(f)

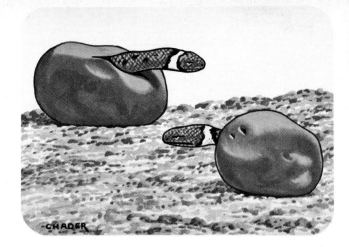

birth. One of these animals just feeds and grows until, at a certain size, it begins to narrow at its middle. This "waist" gets slimmer and slimmer. In a little while the animalcule divides into two. Each half of what had been a single animal is now a small new animal on its own which, in its turn, will become capable of dividing (if it survives) into two individuals—and so on.

Childhood is a term that only has any meaning when applied to creatures to which existence is more than a merely physical routine directed towards the survival of the individual animal. And childhood, together with all the more important things we associate with it, such as parental care and affection, training and play—which is often a special form of training for adult life—becomes recognizably closer and closer to that of a human child as we study more highly developed animals. These are the species which live more complex lives; and for them some form of real childhood is essential.

(above, left)
By the time **baby snakes** hatch from their eggs, their mother is usually long gone, never to return. Neither the eggs nor the young snakes, however, need her care or protection. The eggs are tough and rubbery and the baby snakes are prepared to start life on their own as soon as they enter the world.

(above)
These **crocodile eggs** lie together on the sand near water. From now on Nature will be their only mother.

Snake Babies Are Deserted by Mother

IF YOU HAPPENED TO COME UPON a litter of baby snakes just hatching from their eggs, in a sheltered place in the lee of a big stone or an old stump, you might instinctively glance around expecting to see the mother snake somewhere nearby, watching out for her youngsters' welfare. You would be unlikely to find her. Snakes don't "mother" their babies. Very often, the kinds of snakes that lay eggs do not even bother to remain with the eggs to protect them until they are ready to hatch; and the eggs themselves need less protection than the eggs of birds. They are tough, resilient, rubbery things that would bounce, rather than break, if you dropped them. The mother snake is liable to glide away from them forever as soon as they are laid, leaving them to be hatched by time and the sun. Even those snakes which bring forth their young alive hardly stay with their babies for longer than it takes to

Life is difficult for young animals whose parents do not care for them, and many do not live. In order for these species to survive, the young must be born in very large **broods**, out of which only a fraction may live. Birds, on the other hand, have a true childhood season with personal mothering, and their broods can be quite small. Many broods have only four or five chicks or even less. This one, for example, consists of just three **young owls**.

set them down into the world "on their own". Within seconds after its life begins, a little snake is ready to use the instinctive technique of coiling and striking; no less important—and this is something to remember—baby snakes of poisonous species are equipped from the start with fangs and venom, and the instinct to use them effectively.

Turtle Babies Have Only Mother Nature to Guide Them

AMONG OTHER BABIES "born old" are turtles, lizards and most fishes. As the naturalist John Burroughs expressed it, lives like these—destined to be lived almost entirely according to instinct, in a limited kind of environment, with relatively few and simple adjustments to be made—can do without mothering because "Nature is mother enough for them." A baby turtle hatching from its egg, shallowly buried in the sand or mud of the shore, emerges with an instinctive knowledge that it must go uphill. This brings it safely out of its birthplace. Once this has been accomplished the turtle, just as automatically, heads for the nearby water. These are natural responses which, without any mother's guidance, ensure the young creature's immediate survival. Similarly simple responses will guide the turtle through its long, rather dim life.

A Mother Bird Is Devoted to Her Nestling

THE LIVES OF BIRDS ARE VERY DIFFERENT, and it is easy to see that for them there has to be a true childhood. Somehow the helpless, blind nestling has to be transformed into a mature adult bird with powers of flight and song, highly specialized feeding skills and an ability to defend itself against enemies. In bird life we find mothers who are dedicated parents. The chick can really be compared, without too great a strain on the imagination, with a baby. A relatively long period of its life will be spent in developing its individuality and its skill in the business of living. Although some of its skills are instinctive and seem to "come naturally" when they are needed, it will also learn from its parents.

Parents Who Neglect Children Must Have More Babies

WHERE NATURE SERVES AS THE ONLY "PARENT", great numbers of youngsters die very soon after coming into being. But under this impersonal scheme, the survival of the species is generally assured by the size of the brood. A mother fish has to lay hundreds of thousands of eggs. In many species, such as cod, the number may run to five or ten million. Insects often produce huge broods; common garter snakes

(bottom left)
It is a mystery how they know where to go, but soon after **baby snapping turtles** hatch from a "clutch" of eggs, they find their way to the nearest river or lake. Instinct is evidently enough to get them off to a start in life and to guide them from then on, without any help from a mother. Adult snapping turtles weigh up to sixty pounds and have jaws like steel traps.

(bottom right)
From nest-building to feeding and flight-training, birds care for their young with great effort and attention. Since a baby bird can eat an amount of food equal to its own weight every twenty-four hours, bird parents may be busy all day long searching for food and bringing it back to their nests to satisfy their hungry nestlings. One mother **wren** made 1,214 meal trips in a single day.

may give birth to thirty or forty or more babies in a litter. The batch of little tadpoles hatching from egg-masses their mother has deposited in a springtime pond may number anything from several hundred to over ten thousand!

Among the birds, however, where there has come to be a true season of childhood, with personal mothering, many species have only four or five youngsters in a brood, and many have fewer. A dove, for instance, has only two chicks. So does the tiny hummingbird. The condor, one of the biggest flying land birds in the world, has just a single chick, which will enjoy what is probably the most prolonged of all bird childhoods; the baby condor takes two years to develop from a helpless infant into a fully competent adult.

The Wren That Served 1,214 Meals a Day

BIRDS CARE FOR THEIR OFFSPRING with attention and pains at every stage of their upbringing. Most of us have seen at least some of the many intricate kinds of nests that serve as nurseries for their young as well as homes for themselves. Perhaps we have watched the process of family care and "mothering". While a mother bird broods her eggs, she turns them regularly every day, sometimes twice a day, assuring that they are evenly warmed. The parent bird will frequently help the young chick out of the shell, and as soon as the process is complete will carry away the now useless shell to make the nest neat and clean. As her babies grow, she feeds them with almost unbelievable frequency; often life for both bird parents becomes little more than an exhausting series of trips in search of food and back to the nest, as

Young **western grebes** may ride around on the back of their mother or father or take shelter under a parent's wing. Grebes are not good flyers but they can expel air from their bodies and sink quietly below the surface of the water if danger threatens. Freshwater lakes and ponds are their usual habitat.

long as daylight lasts. A baby bird can eat the equivalent of its own
weight every twenty-four hours. Such an appetite makes a tremendous
demand on the parents, but birds are equal to it. Arthur A. Allen, the
ornithologist, reported the case of a mother wren whose feeding trips
to her babies were carefully counted between sunrise and darkness one
day. During that period, she brought morsels to her little ones 1,214
times! In contrast to this, an eagle may visit the nest only two or three
times a day; but each time it brings in a huge amount of food that will
give the youngsters the opportunity of feeding themselves over a period of several hours.

It is more difficult to measure the amount of food which birds such
as honeyeaters and hummingbirds provide for their young; this food is

a liquid composed mainly of flower nectar and semi-dissolved insects. The astounding rate of growth of the young gives us some idea of the enormous amount of food they consume; one species increases in weight fifty-fold within just three weeks!

Birds Need Long, Patient Training

THE SERVICE OF BIRDS to their children includes tirelessly carrying away dirt and muss from the nest; perching patiently on the nest-rim with outstretched wings to shield the babies from sun or rain; teaching them how to recognize natural enemies by giving warning cries and making a commotion when one comes too close to the nest. The parents coax the young birds into flight when they are physically capable of it; the golden eagle induces its young to take to the air by dropping tidbits of food at increasing distances from the nest. Among songbirds, the use of the voice to produce the song of the species is something that calls for a skill that must be learned; and it is largely learned by example. Naturalists have found that a feeble broken little song is the best that can be achieved by a songbird which has been reared without the benefit of the family influence that is normal among its species.

Though birds' care of their youngsters is largely instinctive and

(below)
Short-eared owls are often seen by casual observers because they hunt by day as well as by night. The nest is on the ground, hidden only by the parents' natural camouflage. Protection from natural enemies as well as from sun and rain are part of a bird's tireless service to its young.

(above)
While ponds, marshes and lakes are the favored environment of **mallards,** or wild ducks, the female builds her nest on land and lines it with feathers plucked from her breast. About a dozen ducklings make up her brood, which she leads right to the water and seems able to care for without any trouble. After about two months the half-grown ducks can fly and are ready to go off on their own.

"compulsive", and probably has little to do with awareness or intelligence, it shows a close foreshadowing of the kind of devotion that marks the relationship of parents to their young among the highest animals of all, the mammals, and especially among human beings.

Birds Make Splendid Foster Parents

A BIRD MOTHER'S ATTACHMENT to her eggs is so strong and deep that if the eggs are taken away from a brooding gull, for instance, she will "mother" a ping-pong ball, a matchbox, or almost any small object offered to her. Affection towards nestlings is even fiercer. Parent birds have such a deeply felt impulse to look after youngsters that they may undertake to feed and raise any abandoned fledgling in their vicinity. Among birds that live in flocks or communities, this broadened devotion is often touchingly shown. Oriental bird-dealers sometimes impose the care of as many as fifty baby finches on a single pair of finch adults. The grown birds weary themselves to exhaustion, eager to look after them all. Solicitude for abandoned eggs or orphaned youngsters perhaps reaches its height in penguins. Penguins will cluster by the dozen around a stray egg and will sometimes fight among themselves for the privilege of brooding it; and when a penguin chick is orphaned the whole colony of birds is ready to serve as its foster parents.

But it is among the mammals that we find nature's creatures protecting their children, helping to elicit their developing instincts and giving them training for grown-up life, in ways that closely parallel the parent-child relations of human beings. But animals are not "people", and we should always remember this when studying animals and seeking

The North American **blue jay** likes open forest but also takes up residence in city parks and suburbs. Like all members of the crow family, it builds a sizable nest of sticks, which may appear rather loosely put together. It robs the nests of other birds but protects its own by building it among dense foliage.

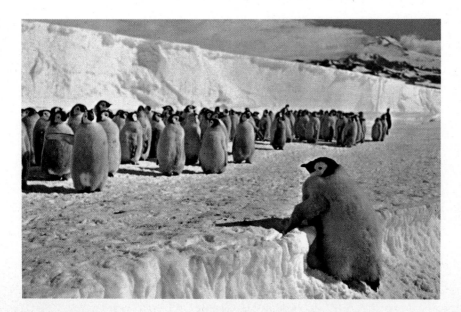

Among birds that live in flocks or colonies, a type of community child-raising often occurs. In this picture several adult **emperor penguins** guard the large nursery, while the other adults may be off somewhere else. A stray egg or an abandoned or orphaned penguin chick will be adopted by the whole colony. Though particularly strong in penguins, such **devotion to young** other than their own is not uncommon among birds.

to understand them; we should not make the mistake of what naturalists call *anthropomorphism*—reading too much of our human kind of personality into any non-human life, or applying human standards to animals that are in fact very different from humans. If we could somehow get inside an animal, and experience things the way it does, life would undoubtedly seem quite different to us as a result.

A Dog Smells Its World

DOGS HAVE BEEN ASSOCIATES of man for so long that we think of them almost as members of the human family; every day we see resemblances between them and ourselves—and forget their relationship to such wild animals as wolves and foxes which means that the most "human" canine mother, proudly bringing up her pups, is introducing them to a life significantly different from ours in many ways. Theirs will be a life in which "thought" and reflection will have only a very minor part, and which will be governed by spontaneous animal response to instinct and the impulse of the moment. Their world even looks different from ours; it is a world of black, white and greys, because their eyes cannot distinguish hues—only tones. But if it is a life in which seeing means less than it does to us it is also one in which smelling means a great deal more. We can no more imagine the vivid range of sensations revealed to a dog in its highly developed olfactory sense than a polar bear can imagine the landscape of the Amazon jungle. In a famous scientific experiment some years ago it was found that a dog's nose is so keen it can detect the presence of iodoform in a solution of one part to four million. It can detect this trace of a scent even when it has been disguised with four or five other powerful scents intermixed. An animal with such a sense must, irrespective of intelligence, experience the world in quite different terms from our own.

An animal's world cannot be exactly like ours; but it is not so different as not to allow us to see many points of similarity. The similarities to, and the contrasts with, our own kind of childhood that we can detect among "animal children" can help to establish a feeling of kinship with other creatures, and a sympathy which will be the better for not being "anthropomorphic".

Baby-Carriage, a Kangaroo Invention!

EVERY BABY NEEDS protection if it is to survive. It needs a sheltered place where the mother can look after it. What birds achieve by building a nest for their babies, the animals called marsupials manage by means of a *portable* nursery, a sort of internal one. "Marsupial" means "pouched". There are three particularly famous animals of this kind: kangaroos, koalas and opossums. They are the logical animals

(above)
This Australian **dingo pup** is actually a wild animal, which is probably descended from an ancient breed of Asian dog. A dog has an extremely keen **sense of smell** and can detect many scents that we aren't aware of.

(above)
Coyote pups resemble domestic dogs and are full of curiosity. The father plays an important part in their upbringing.

for us to talk about first, because they represent in the animal world a stage in the slow transition from an egg-laying way of life to the way of the highest mammals. In the kangaroo, koala and opossum, the more primitive egg-laying style of reproduction is replaced by the egg-retention pattern that prevails among all the higher animals; but the baby comes into the world woefully little prepared for external existence.

The kangaroo is a native of Australasia. The female has on the lower part of her body a big, deep "pocket", a pouch that has a circular ribbon of muscle around its mouth so that she can either draw it almost completely closed or open it wide. If it were not for this furry receptacle in which her baby can be stored after birth, the mother kangaroo could not possibly succeed in child rearing. Although a fully grown male kangaroo is taller than a man and weighs around 200 pounds, it is born only about five weeks after being conceived, and is then a good deal less than one inch long. In fact, the incompletely formed little mite is so tiny that two or three like him could lie together in a teaspoon!

Without its mother's protective **pouch,** the tiny, blind and helpless newborn **kangaroo** could not survive. Even inside the warm, furry pouch the infant kangaroo has no power to feed itself by sucking, and the mother has to pump her milk into it. After several months it will be seen peeping out of its "baby-carriage" at the world as the mother hops along on her hind legs. There are special muscles around the mouth of the pouch that allow the mother to open or close it. This pouch is the distinguishing feature of all the animals known as **marsupials.**
A small species of kangaroo, the **yellow-footed wallaby,** is shown in the picture at the right (above).

How the Newborn "Joey" Is Fed

THE PINK, BLIND AND TOTALLY HELPLESS newborn kangaroo is such a "premature" baby that its body is actually semi-transparent, like an earthworm's. The only part of the baby kangaroo that is well developed and strong are its front feet. Just as soon as the tiny "Joey" is ushered into life, it grips its mother's fur with all its might and, guided by instinct, starts hitching its way toward the protective pouch on her abdomen. Ordinarily, no help is needed in this first adventure; but, if necessary, the mother will take the baby carefully in her lips and tuck it away inside her pouch. This will be its own private warm, furry world for some time to come, because only one kangaroo is born at a time.

Many of the lower animals spend little or no time with a parent and must be able to fend for themselves as soon as they are born. **Snakes,** for example, may come into the world alone or be deserted by their mother almost immediately. It is a different matter with animals that need parental care at birth, especially mammals. Among the smallest of the true mammals, **shrews** are born in litters of from five to ten young and are nursed by the mother. The adults are well-known for their bad tempers and enormous appetites. On the other hand, the **walrus** is more sociable. A mother walrus gives birth to one or two calves, which are big even at birth and wrinkled like an adult. The young are nursed for almost two years and may ride on their mother's back as she swims through the water.

As soon as the young kangaroo is installed in the pouch, it takes hold of the mother's milk gland and hangs on with an unbreakable grip. Yet the infant kangaroo has no power to feed itself by sucking; the mother kangaroo actually pumps milk into the baby by using a special set of muscles.

We may wonder how the young kangaroo can manage to breathe and avoid choking, with milk continually being pumped into its gullet as it jounces along in its nursery. The explanation is that the nursling kangaroo has a specially adapted breathing apparatus, by which air can pass directly into the lungs via a passage having no direct connection with the mouth or gullet.

Four months after birth, a kangaroo youngster has grown a coat of fur and detached itself from the constant milk supply; and it will be spending a good deal of time peeping at the world from the safety of the pouch. This is a scene almost all of us have probably seen in pictures or cartoons. When the Joey's mother halts to graze, it clambers out, hops to the ground and starts some nibbling on its own; but at any sign of danger, the youngster makes a rush for the pouch and dives in head-first; then it must scramble around in order to get right-side-up again.

The Kangaroo's Amazing Leaping Powers

GRADUALLY THE JOEY grows up. It takes to hopping along beside the mother for longer and longer periods, strengthening its legs in the leaping skill that enables a grown kangaroo to make a thirty-foot broad jump or a sailing arc over a ten-foot fence. Only when really serious danger threatens now does it still take refuge in the

SHREW

WALRUS

SNAKE

pouch and let itself be borne away on a bounding flight to safety. If the mother should be run down and captured, the Joey is very unlikely to be captured too, because a mother kangaroo's strategy when she finds herself hard pressed is to lift her baby out of her pocket and tumble it into a hiding place as she races and leaps along. If she finally manages to escape her pursuers she will quietly return to retrieve her waiting offspring.

The Australian Teddy Bear

ANOTHER CELEBRATED AUSTRALIAN marsupial, the koala, is a slow, gentle, woolly-coated animal that loves to clamber around in eucalyptus trees. The Teddy bear was designed after the image of the little koala, at the prompting of Theodore (Teddy) Roosevelt, former President of the United States. The mother koala has a baby, as a rule, at intervals of two years—just a single baby, like the kangaroo. Unlike the kangaroo, the little koala stays in its fur-lined cradle only a short time, until the mother transfers it to her furry back. There the young koala spends its whole childhood, riding or taking climbing lessons by cautiously hitching its way around to her underside and back up again. Koalas are as mild and gentle as they look and the baby's growing up has a placid slowness in keeping with the quality of koala life. The young koala continues to cling to its mother until it is almost half as big as she is. When it comes time for the baby to be weaned from a milk diet to eucalyptus leaves—the food which full-grown koalas eat exclusively—the mother helps it through the transition by one of the strangest features in any animal childhood. Her body develops a temporary power to make eucalyptus "pap". This "vegetable

In contrast to the walrus calf, the **bear** cub is a tiny, toothless infant at birth, often weighing less than a pound. When the mother bear is still hibernating, the cubs are born— usually one or two—and she nurses them while she remains in her winter den. If a cub from a previous year is still with her, it will help raise the new babies. We turn to the **elephant,** however, for an even greater contrast in size. Every two years the mother can give birth, usually to a single calf. The newborn elephant may weigh 200 pounds and stand three feet tall. After several hours it can stand, and two days later it is able to walk. For about two years it will continue to enjoy the mother's sweet, rich milk, even after it has started to eat grass.

ELEPHANT

BEAR

soup", as one naturalist calls it, is produced only for a month or so, every two or three days, and only at a special time in the afternoon.

Baby 'Possums Often Come in Dozen Lots

AMERICAN OPOSSUMS are animals as slow and placid as their marsupial koala cousins. When an opossum is born it is smaller than an acorn, much smaller as a matter of fact than a newborn squirrel. Unlike the kangaroo and koala, this is not a solitary baby but one of a brood that may number as many as a dozen. At birth, the baby hitches its way to the mother's pouch and snuggles in as one of a host of brothers and sisters. The young opossum stays six or seven weeks in the warm security of the pouch, suckling, dozing, growing a silky down of soft fur, presently opening bright little black eyes. As the opossum children grow, the portable nursery becomes seriously over-crowded—elastic though the pouch is. Cautiously at first, then more ven-turesomely, the youngsters take to peeping out of the pouch opening. Then, like the baby koala, they climb out onto their mother's back. On either side of her backbone they cling in rows, their sharp little chins hooked over the ridge to steady them, their strong-thumbed little hands holding fast to her fur.

Now and again the mother opossum arches her strong tail, almost a foot long, up over her back. At this signal, the opossum children wrap the tips of their own little tails around her big strong one and hang from it upside down. The prehensile skill of their tails, learned this way, will be useful to them in adult life, as will the flexible strength of their small thumbs, perfected in clinging to the mother's back and shaggy coat. Joggling, swaying, watching with bright little black eyes the exciting and mysterious forest world, the young opossums ride their maternal caravan.

(top)
These **koala bears,** are slow, gentle animals that feed on eucalyptus leaves. The baby koala stays in its mother's pouch for a short time and then spends the rest of its childhood riding and climbing around on her back, until it is half-grown. The mother weans it from its milk diet with a eucalyptus "pap" that she makes—a sort of "vegetable soup."

(above)
American **black bears** often have twins, which are only about the size of a rat when born. Sometimes one twin is black and the other brown.

Out into the World

OPOSSUMS DO NOT STAY with the mother as long as the koala does. They have not only large families, but frequent ones. While the youthful passengers are still enjoying themselves, riding on the mother's back, a new generation of tiny babies is already growing in the warm pouch. Mother begins to be impatient with her "teen-age" passengers. She takes to nipping at them, shaking herself to break their grip on her fur and tail. Before long opossum striplings heed the increasingly vigorous messages telling them their childhood must be put behind them. One by one, in the dusk of a summer evening, they climb down for the last time and slip away into the dark woods to begin the adventure of "life on their own".

Young animals that do not enjoy the protection of their mothers' con-tinual presence may be protected in other ways. There are three chief means. The baby may be born in such a good hiding-place—a high treetop nest, an underground burrow, a concealed hillside den—that it can safely be left unwatched in the mother's absence. If the nursery is not of such a completely sheltering kind as this, the baby animal may be dressed in a protectively camouflaged coat. Alternatively, a baby may form so completely during the period in its mother's body before birth—the period of gestation—that it will already be far from helpless when it enters the world.

Bats are rather amazing mammals, so we need not be surprised to find unusual habits in the way they care for their young. In almost all cases, the young are able to hang onto the mother's fur with a very tight grip almost as soon as they are born. The mother commonly flies about with one, two, three or even four young, tightly clamped against her belly. Sometimes she is able to do this even when the young weigh more than herself. This will seem the more remarkable if you consider the rapid dives, climbs and changes of direction necessary in catching insects "on the wing" and the vast numbers of them that must be needed to sustain such an active warm-blooded creature.

Bats vary tremendously in their habits. Some are definitely diurnal, flying about in broad daylight, while others emerge from roosting-places only after full darkness has set in. Some species have never been seen feeding, for this very reason. Some hibernate, hanging up in a protected spot and apparently not even moving for six or seven months, while others migrate southward to spend the winter. The habits of most species fall somewhere in the middle and involve a hibernation period of medium length. Some species live in the far recesses of caves, perhaps a mile from the entrance; others sleep in the open, on rocks, on the sides of buildings, or in bushes. One thing bats seem to have in common is the way in which they care for the young, carrying them about, clinging to the parent's fur, until they become too large. They are then left in roosts, and visited by the mother for fairly frequent feedings until they no longer need such care and are ready to set out on their own.

Horse and Deer Young Can Walk at Birth

ANYONE WHO HAS SPENT TIME on a farm may have seen how soon a little foal is able to get to its feet. Within minutes after coming into the world, it can stand beside its mother, rather shaky and tottery, to be sure, but still able to keep its footing on its long, spindly legs. Almost all the horse's wild relatives are similarly quick to "get their bearings" in babyhood. A newborn baby zebra will be on its feet about

A young deer, or **fawn,** can walk almost immediately after it is born. Since it is defenseless, though, its best protection is to lie very still and close to the ground. When it does, its spotted coat blends with the pattern of sunlight and leaf shadows of wooded areas, so that it practically "vanishes."

Even when the young kangaroo, or **Joey,** is ready to leave the mother's pouch for short periods, it uses it as a retreat for as much as a year. When frightened it will make a dash for the pouch, diving in head-first.

This zebra group is standing near a **water hole,** a place that naturally attracts all sorts of animals in the dry areas of Africa. The animals arrive in the evening and through the night, leaving in the early hours of the morning, before the day gets hot.

About five minutes after being born, a baby **zebra** is on its feet, and in little more than an hour it may be tottering after its mother, hungering for milk. The mare does not give birth every year and she only has one baby at a time.

The type of zebra pictured here, the Grevy (or Grévy's) zebra, is the largest and most northern of the zebras. Its ears are longer and stripes narrower than those of the other species.

five minutes after being born, and can totter after the mother, begging for milk, within an hour or so. Tapir babies are extremely prompt toddlers. So are rhinoceros youngsters, even though their childhood is a long one, lasting five or six years.

The animal the Americans call a moose (which in Asia and Europe is called an elk) is not only the largest deer of North America; it is an animal of impressive size by any standard. Adult bulls can reach 1,800 pounds. Adult cows usually weigh from 600 to 800 pounds, and even a newborn calf from twenty to twenty-five. Calves, born with their eyes open and with a respectable coat of fur, can walk within a few hours. After such a quick start, it is a little surprising to learn that they suckle for six months to a year before they drift away to forage on their own; they will actually be driven away, if the cow is expecting another calf.

Among other advanced animal babies are antelopes and chamois. A newborn chamois can walk around, slowly but sure-footedly, even before it has dried off in the strange air and sunshine of its new world. Many other animals of different kinds belong among the comparatively precocious babies. One of the most comical is a baby porcupine. Its bristly mother, armed with upward of 25,000 quills, weighs only twelve or thirteen pounds; but the little porky comes into the world weighing a full pound, shadowed with a stubble of quills that start growing promptly, and within a couple of days of its birth the young animal will be climbing trees and nibbling at leaves and twigs!

This **American elk** calf and its mother may be crossing the stream or pausing for a moment in the middle of it. The cow elk gives birth in the spring and nurses her calf until the autumn. When it is about six months old, this calf's spots will disappear and it will take on the same coloring as an adult. American elk are closely related to the European red deer.

Safe Hidden Nurseries for Less Mature Babies

LESS ADVANCED ANIMAL BABIES are given the protection of many kinds of nurseries. Baby woodchucks and baby badgers start their childhoods in a dark, cozy nursery-room of an underground burrow. So do baby chipmunks, baby gophers and many others. A mother weasel outfits a nursery in a stone-heap or a hollow log. A mother white-footed mouse likes to find an old abandoned bird's nest, often a thrush's or catbird's, which can be enlarged and roofed with dried leaves and grasses to make a warm, snug house in the heart of which is the nursery lined with soft mosses and shreds of cedar bark. Nurseries for baby beavers and baby muskrats are in the "lodges" the adults make; or else in deep bank-side burrows that lead to a roomy chamber about a yard wide with a foot-high ceiling, which may be as far as thirty feet back from the burrow's opening. Fox cubs first open their eyes in April in what is called an "earth"—a tunneled den in the ground, often an enlarged and made-over house that was originally

(top left)
The intelligent **elephant** lives in a well-ordered society, in which the calf will be cared for by foster mothers if disaster befalls its natural mother.

(top right)
A few minutes after it is born, a baby **colt** can get to its feet and stand beside its mother. Though shaky, it manages to keep its footing.

(above, left)
Young **hedgehogs** have spines, but, unlike the adults, they cannot roll themselves up into a ball for protection.

(above, right)
The calf of a **domestic cow** can stand and—unlike its placid mother—it is very active.

the burrow of some other animal. The mother cottontail rabbit, one of the most familiar animals to all of us who go into the fields, prepares for her babies a shallow hollow in the ground, lined with grasses and leaves. Hidden among the tall stems of the meadow grass, the nest is concealed by a blanket-like covering of fur from the mother's own body. Among the animals whose babies are born very helpless, and must be hidden securely for a long while, there are ingenious nurseries to fit every need.

Midway between these animal children that have sheltering nests and the precocious ones whose parents need make no such provision are the babies whose protection comes largely from their special markings. Grown-up lions have tawny coats, but a baby lion is all mottled with an array of spots, and its tail shows a clear trace of dark circling rings. Mountain lions, or pumas, are almost uniformly reddish-tawny, but a puma cub in babyhood is strikingly splashed and dappled with markings: a broad band on each side of its face, spots on its legs and underneath on its chest and belly. A striking instance of the difference between an animal's "baby clothes" and its grown-up dress can be observed in bobcats. The soft, thick fur of an adult bobcat is a light grey, grizzled with rufous brown, with just a very faint trace of some dusky spottings around its mouth, head and tail. But a bobcat kitten is powdered with a dotting of speckles almost all over.

Tiger cubs that are a few days old, on the other hand, will already be marked with the same stripes that they will wear all their lives. Tiger kits, like most other young cats, are fuzzy little bundles of curiosity, unsteady on their feet and with disproportionately large heads. The adults are rarities in the cat world because they not only don't mind water, but seem to delight in bathing when they have an opportunity, and swim readily and quite well. These striking animals most likely originated in northern Asia, and have gradually spread to warmer southern climates. The fact that they can often be seen bathing in hot weather suggests that they "feel the heat" more than the other big cats; perhaps because they are not, even yet, quite so well adapted to life in very warm climates.

Naturalists think that markings that are peculiar to the young of a species may "echo" an appearance formerly common to the adult, also, in an earlier epoch.

How a Baby Fawn Learns to Be "Invisible"

ALONE IN THE SPRING UNIVERSE into which it has newly come, a little fawn crouches in a hollowed form of grasses. It lies very, very still. Adults of its kind measure six feet in length, stand three feet high at the shoulder, and may weigh nearly two hundred pounds; but a baby fawn is tiny. When it stands (which it cannot do anything like as expertly as a very young foal can), it is a scant

During the bitter Antarctic winter, the **penguin** balances its single egg on top of its foot to insulate it from the frozen ground. Later, the chick is held the same way.

Fox cubs usually come in twos, fours or even sixes. They are left alone while their parents hunt, but they stay close to their den. The father fox is a model parent, providing food, chewing it for the cubs, and later training them in the skills and cunning they need to survive.

Tiger cubs have the same markings as the grown adult, and like all kittens they are playful and full of curiosity. Tigers like to bathe and are good swimmers.

Selecting an old abandoned bird's nest, a mother **white-footed mouse** (or deer mouse) will enlarge it and roof it with dried leaves and grasses to make a home for her babies. The young are tiny when born, but they grow quickly and are usually darker than their parents. White-footed mice are very clean and orderly and are among the commonest animals in North America.

(top left)

Fox cubs are nursed in an underground den, called an **"earth,"** which is often an old burrow dug by some other animal and enlarged by the vixen, or mother fox. In the spring the cubs come outside for the first time.

(top right)

The **baby fawn** is weak and unsteady on its legs, but the many spots on its coat help it to hide from its enemies. It soon learns to follow the flashing white guiding signal of its mother's tail as she slips quietly through the leafy woods.

sixteen inches tall and weighs only about five pounds. From soon after the time of its birth, its mother, the doe, will quite often leave it alone for rather long periods. The woods-world has its dangers for a helpless little fawn. So its way is to lie exceedingly still, with its slim legs tucked in close to its body. Hugging the ground, motionless, the baby fawn gives off very little betraying scent. Its protection against sharp eyes is its coat; so long as it remains motionless its dappled hide blends with the sun-flecked pattern of the leaves and in an almost magical way the quiet little youngster "disappears".

Whether it begins life almost helpless like the baby piglets that must be carefully guarded and prodigiously fed by their mother for almost two weeks, or whether it begins life with the kind of "head start" that enables a baby hippopotamus to know how to swim even before it knows how to walk, an animal youngster has a great deal to learn. Unless we have had some reason to study the matter, we may easily fail to realize how much.

How the White-tailed Deer Signals Safety and Danger

THE LITTLE WHITE-TAILED FAWN, lying with slim legs tucked under it in its concealing thicket, its great dark eyes watching the wonders of the green world, must even have lessons in that art of stillness which is its chief source of safety. Often when it hears its mother coming, it struggles to its feet and wobbles eagerly to meet her; and often when she is leaving it, and it still feels hungry and lonesome, it tries to follow her on insecure legs. She bunts and pushes it with her head, forcing it down. These lessons continue until it has learned obedience. Later, when the fawn is stronger and ready to make trips from home, she bleats softly and teaches it to understand the signal-flagging of her tail. A deer's tail is nearly a foot long and rather bushy. When held downward, pressed against her body, it is brown, like the rest of the deer's coat—and inconspicuous; but when it is

raised it shows the flashing white of its underside. This carries a message for the youngster, who learns to watch for that quick white glimmer among the tree trunks. It means "Get up! Come! Follow me!" The young fawn learns to bound forward, trot from cover, and to follow where the mother leads. After that, travelling, exploring, it learns more and more. What the coughing deer-cry means, how to respond to the bark that means urgent danger; what different kinds of twig-snapping signify; what is the safe way by which a band of deer can cross a highway. The best way of road-crossing, a little white-tail learns, is for one member of the herd, usually a doe, to advance to within a few yards of the roadside while all the others hold back. The advance doe stops, looks and listens. If all seems well, she flirts her tail vigorously, showing the white signal-flag. Then she walks slowly and alertly forward to the road's edge, and the rest of the herd advances to where she was previously standing. At the roadside she again pauses, looks carefully both ways, raises her signal-flag, then vaults across the road. Reaching the far side, she makes one final reconnoiter. Then she gives her white flag a last triumphant flip. "All's well! Come ahead!", and the herd goes trooping across the road.

Baby Swans Avoid Water

WHEN WE SEE how gracefully and naturally swans glide around on a pond or lake, it is easy to believe that these creatures must have an inborn predilection—but not so. A baby swan, called a cygnet, must be coaxed and wheedled to take to the water and, once in, will make frantic efforts to get out of it, either by "escaping" to the bank or by climbing up on its mother's safe, dry back. Young swans may stay with their parents for nine months; during this time they are taught many things and receive the almost undivided attention of one or both parents. Despite the fact that the cygnets can feed themselves almost as soon as they hatch, they are very well cared for, and are

(top)
Strange as the **wildebeest,** or **gnu,** may appear, its behavior can be even more unusual. For no apparent reason one will kick up its heels, buck, gallop off, turn around and cavort in general. Notwithstanding, wildebeests are good parents to their one or two young.

(above)
Camels with two humps and long hair, like this **young Bactrian camel,** are very numerous throughout Asia, north of the Himalayas. Blizzards don't bother them at all. Big humps are an indication of good health.

frequently carried around on a parent's back. They may nestle down between the wings, or under one, and peek out from their warm retreat. Certainly this is one of the most appealing "family groups" in the avian world. The stateliness of the swan alone is impressive, the cygnets are most attractive in their fuzzy coats of down, and these plus the enormous size difference between the two make a sight that could not fail to impress anyone.

It sometimes comes as a surprise to find just how many of an animal's "simplest" and most "natural" activities that could easily be supposed to be wholly instinctive are actually things that have to be learned. When we see a hen and chicks all pecking happily in a barnyard, we may think that a chick automatically knows how to feed itself. But it must learn. A baby chick first pecks at everything it finds. It picks up pebbles, sticks, bits of grass—anything at all. Only by childish trial-and-error does it learn what is good to eat. As a matter of fact, a baby chick does not even know how to drink. It makes the great discovery of water in the course of pecking away at all sorts of shiny things—and learns how to quench its thirst!

A Baby Seal Must Be Taught to Swim!

A HARBOR SEAL is as much at home in the water as a fish. Seals live on rocky promontories around bays, loving to bask on the rocks in the sunlight when they are not cavorting in the water. When the time comes for a mother seal to have a baby, she usually swims far up a river, and the baby is born some distance from the open sea. It is a sleek, chubby and uncommonly winsome baby, its first fur a soft white, later a sort of dappled yellow-grey with variegated spottings. It loves the warm sunlight and the company of its mother—a colony of nursling seals is a continual uproar of plaintive *wa-a-aa's* as the youngsters complain of their mothers' absences—and it loves milk, which it will drink for about a month before taking an interest in fish. What it does not like is the water. Seal pups learning to be water-wise are a delightful spectacle. Mother takes the pup to the edge of the rocks, nudges it, nuzzles it and urges it tenderly. No result. She tries again, coaxing, pleading, slipping sleekly into the water herself and gliding around to show what fun it is. No. She flippers her way back up onto the rocks again and approaches the pup. This time, there is no pleading; with an adroit shove, she tumbles the little one into the water. Thrashing and spluttering, the baby seal for a few minutes seems all outraged misery. It hurries back up onto the rocks. But then, come to think of it, that plunge *was* fun. It peeks over the rock edge at the water, hitches a bit closer, and suddenly—splash!—has made a dive on its own. It has made the grand initiation into being a grown-up seal. It is an initiation which is made with almost as much timidity and reluctance by the seal's huge relative, the Arctic walrus. A baby walrus is destined to grow

(below)
Young **moose** calves are as ungainly-looking as their parents, but they seem to be fascinated by every new thing they see or meet—including skunks and porcupines! They grow rapidly and will weigh about 400 pounds when a year old.

(bottom)
At birth a **seal pup** has its eyes open and wears a good coat of white fur, but it is still rather helpless. After six or eight weeks this Alaskan fur seal pup will be an expert swimmer, but at first the mother has all she can do just to get it into the water.

Pelicans may look clumsy on land, but they are excellent flyers and swimmers. The chicks, however, are helpless, and the parents patiently care for them until they are ready to fly. Usually this occurs when they are about two months old.

up to an adult weight of over a ton, which it will sustain by eating over a hundred pounds of fish every day; but in childhood the strapping youngster is sometimes as uneasy about the water as its little seal cousin. Grunting, pushing and straining, the mother walrus has to heave her enormous but terrified baby over the edge of the ice floe into the dark, forbidding current.

Course in Aeronautics for Squirrels!

A SIMILAR ADVENTURE, but in a different element, marks the childhood of young flying squirrels. They must overcome fear, not of water, but of the air. A flying squirrel cannot really fly; but it has a web of furry skin stretching between forelegs and hind legs, and when it spreads out all four limbs the skin is extended to become something like a pair of wings. On these the squirrel can glide through the air, on a downward slant, sailing from a treetop to a slightly lower point on another tree a hundred feet or more away. Flying squirrels are gentle, playful, shy little animals, active almost exclusively at night. The babies are often born in a snug hollow of an old tree. Gradually they must learn to make excursions from the nest, climbing around on the tree trunk and in the branches; but there is no *gradual* way to learn such an improbable feat as taking off in a long swooping glide through the empty air.

(below)
A **flying squirrel** has a **web of furry skin** that is stretched between its forelegs and hindlegs. When its limbs are stretched out it can glide from one tree to a slightly lower point on another. A playful, shy little animal, it does most of its flying after dark.

(bottom right)
Black bears are born in the dead of winter, when the mother is in a deep sleep. Still to be found in many parts of North America and especially in the national parks, they live in forests and breed only every two years. Shown here are a mother and her three cubs.

At a nudge from its mother, in the dusk of a summer evening in the woods, the baby flying squirrel suddenly finds itself dislodged from the edge of the tree-hollow and tumbling through space. Instinctively it spreads out its little legs; its soft-furred, broad tail is thrust out straight as a kind of combination rudder and parachute. Suddenly it finds itself sliding smoothly through the air, coasting downhill as serenely as a boy coasting downhill on a sled.

Learning Is Generally Fun for Animal Children

CHILDHOOD FOR ANIMALS is pretty much of a game. There is a lot to learn, but learning can be fun; and the two go together in innumerable kinds of antics that make animals' childhood days an endless pleasure to watch. No animal, even a grown-up one, can have much of the dreary qualities of worry or anxiety in its life, because as we have seen, animals' minds are not so fully developed that they can give much thought to anything beyond the here-and-now of things; but in childhood an animal is particularly happily absorbed in the fun of exploring its expanding powers. The lives of animal children are largely ruled by the spirit of creative play.

A lioness will offer her children the tip of her tail as a plaything, twitching and vibrating it to attract their notice, then moving it slowly or thrashing it quickly as the youngsters make rushing pounces in an attempt to catch it. Many other mothers among the big cats teach hunting skills by the same game. Wildcat kittens, like the kittens of domestic cats, spend hours in frisky rigmaroles that perfect their capabilities for climbing, jumping and pinning down their prey with an adroit forepaw. Little lynxes, no less than house kittens, are great ones for making stiff-legged prances and leaps almost straight up into the air; and they will chase a pebble or twig, batting it with their paws, rolling over, kicking with their hind feet, in a wild game that differs

(above)
Often born in a snug hollow of an old tree, newborn **flying squirrels** are pink, naked and blind, with tiny, ratlike tails. They grow quickly but are in no hurry to take to the air. An unexpected push from the mother may be necessary to send them on the first gliding trip.

Among **lions** and other members of the cat family, the same playfulness that is such a delight to watch is also a way of teaching hunting skills to the young. A lioness makes a game of twitching and thrashing her tail while her cubs make pounces and try to catch it. Lion cubs have spotted coats with rings circling their tails.

not at all from the way a pet kitten will play with a spool or a toy mouse, or even a bit of cloth.

The sheep and cows of our farmyards are staid, sober animals when they grow up; but in young lambs and calves we see the play antics that show the youngsters getting ready for such lives as their ancestors led. They take part in exuberant mimic fights. They butt, buck and jump. A baby lamb is by nature a "lonesome" little animal; it hates to be left by its mother even for a little while. As it grows, the lamb's urge to follow develops into training games of follow-the-leader. They are a preparation for the kind of gregarious life that sheep lead in the wild state. Calves' principal games are playful stampedes. Young puppies rush after each other in circles, each trying to "head off" the other. It is the same training-for-life game played by the wild dogs, the wolves, foxes and coyotes.

When Cubs Play Too Roughly, Mother Bear Spanks in Earnest

ALMOST ALL YOUNG ANIMALS love to tussle and wrestle together, in mock fights that train them for possible serious emergencies in their grown-up days. Animal mothers are generally indulgent towards their youngsters but occasionally the youngsters get so carried away that a stern disciplinary maternal paw has to be used. Bear cubs are particularly likely to become over-enthusiastic in their wrestlings and rumpuses. A baby bear is one of the animals that are born tiny and unready for life, almost as much as a baby koala or baby 'possum. Its mother gives birth while she is still drowsing in her winter den, and it is a tiny, toothless infant often weighing less than one pound. But it grows prodigiously and gets to be one of the most high-spirited youngsters in all outdoors. When a couple of bear cubs get to cuffing and nipping each other too uproariously, mother bear growls a warning. If this is unheeded, she may try a mild tap with a shaggy forepaw. If that fails, she may deliver a whole-hearted swat that tumbles the little fellows head over heels. Animal mothers are patient, but not tolerant of nonsense.

Why Do Raccoons "Dunk" Their Food Before They Eat it?

MUCH OF ANIMAL CHILDREN's playing and learning comes from following the mother and imitating her. Young raccoons are bright-eyed forest children, endlessly curious. They pick up the life-lore they need in the course of evening and night-time excursions, following mother 'coon from their hollow tree den. A 'coon family outing is a charming sight to see; mother trundles solemnly along, at a rolling flat-footed gait like a little bear's, her coonlets following earnestly behind her. Every animal child has its special knowledge and habits to acquire; and little raccoons acquire a particularly odd one. Fishing with mother along the moonlit brook, dipping their paws in the dark

(opposite page)
Like most young animals, **bear cubs** are playful and fun-loving. They are fond of wrestling with each other and are apt to get carried away. When that happens and things get too rough, the mother bear growls a warning and, if necessary, delivers a swat with her paw.

A **skunk family** out on its early evening walk is a sight to be seen. Leading the way is the mother skunk, her big plumy tail waving in the air, and behind her, all in a line, come her children, who look like miniatures of her and who follow her every step, turn or pause. When born, skunks are not much larger than mice, and they stay together with their mothers until they are almost full-grown.

flowing water for frogs and crawfish, they learn the curious 'coon-trick of "dunking" a morsel of food before they eat it. Another family outing procession that is delightful to watch—and rather easier to see, for it often takes place in early evening instead of the deeper darkness that 'coons prefer—is a parade of skunks. With her big plumy tail waving, mother skunk slowly and placidly leads her children through the tall meadow grass. The children, which look just like miniatures of mother, imitate her every turn and detour, her every pause to flip over a flat stone or scratch at a tussock in search of grubs and beetles.

Animal Mothers Take Housekeeping Seriously

MOTHER ANIMALS ARE KEPT BUSY with all sorts of supervisory and protective chores from the minute their children are born until the youngsters are weaned and ready to go their own way. In addition to nursing the babies when they are little, later taking them for learning-walks, overseeing their play and training them for obedience, there are many other child-raising tasks we may not ordinarily think about. For instance, there is nursery-cleaning. This is a big job for many animal parents, especially those like the woodchuck and badger whose children live underground. Every bit of the babies' mess is scrupulously removed so that the children's underground room stays fresh and clean. Again, a mother animal must quite often carry her children from one place to another, as when she removes them from a nest threatened by some danger.

Animal mothers have many different methods of transporting their children. The big cats, as well as the domestic ones, usually carry their young by gripping them by the "scruff of the neck" with their mouths.

When mother bear carries her cub, she takes his whole head into her mouth. It looks suffocatingly dangerous, but the baby never seems to suffer harm. Baby mice on the move cling to their mother's nipples.

But Many Fathers Duck Responsibility

IN OUR TALKING ABOUT ANIMALS' CHILDHOODS, and how they are prepared for life under their mothers' tutelage and protection, almost nothing has been said about animal *fathers*. This may seem strange. The reason is that many animal fathers play no part at all in bringing up a family but, having sired the children, go their own way—either to live a solitary life, or to join a group of fellow males.

However, there are variations to this rule. Among quite a few gregarious animals, the children are attended by their own mother only while they are very small and helpless; later on they are brought together with the adult herd and turned over to the communal guardianship of its adult members. Bison babies enjoy the protection of the whole herd while they are growing up. At any hint of danger, the male elders form a protective ring, lowering their formidable heads. A baby giraffe is under a disadvantage very strange for any child; it cannot cry. Giraffes have no vocal cords, so this youngster can never join the chorus of squalls and wails by which other animal children manage to get parental attention in a hurry. The young giraffe is

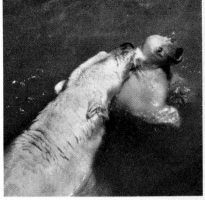

(above)
During the long arctic winter the mother **polar bear** gives birth to her one or two cubs in an ice cave, and in spring she appears with the tiny, sleek-furred young. While polar bears are strong swimmers, the cubs are afraid of the icy waters at first and have to be held up by the mother and taught to swim.

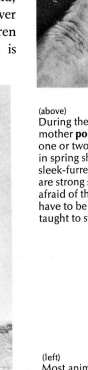

(left)
Most animal babies stay close to mother, but **marmosets**, like this black-plumed youngster, are carried around by father and given to mother only for nursing. Marmosets are small, bright and friendly and have been prized as pets for centuries.

(above)
Like many other squirrels, the North American **grey squirrel** makes its nest in hollow trees or in the topmost branches. Nests, called **"drays,"** are made of leaves and twigs and sometimes reach two feet in diameter.

introduced at the age of a few weeks to a group of youngsters looked after watchfully by older giraffe "nurses". They keep the little fellows rounded up and in order.

Animal Dads Like These Are Models

IT IS IN THOSE ANIMAL FAMILIES where father is an intimate part of the household, sharing the children's feeding and training, that we see the nearest resemblance to human family life. The fatherliness of male animals shines out in the lives of coyotes and foxes. The father is a tireless provider, bringing food to the bright-eyed, wary little cubs waiting in their "earth" or rock-den. In a sense, he even serves as a sort of "nurse", supplementing the milk-nursing the mother provides. When the chubby cubs are old enough to begin needing more solid food than milk, father does not start them on a raw-meat diet abruptly. He partly pre-digests their meals for them, and on returning to the den from hunting trips presents the babies with a sort of soft, chewed-up porridge. Later, father fox or father coyote plays a big part, too, in training the cubs in the wild cunning they will need later. He runs and races with them, helps them sharpen their wits on the problems of the world, and even introduces them to the art of catching prey.

Among monkeys and apes, family life comes to show close and touching resemblances to our own. While mother gorilla is asleep

(right)
This is a very young **stump-tailed macaque,** or red-faced monkey, from Thailand. When not sitting on its tail and bending it out of shape, this monkey is probably waggling it wildly, as if it were saying "Hello."

in a tree-bed with her child, father gorilla makes himself a couch at the foot of a nearby tree, against which he props himself each evening to keep watch over the little household. Protectiveness towards their children is so developed in baboons that not only does mother show endless patient affection in letting her young one ride piggyback, and not only is father fiercely valiant in guarding his offspring, but even the baby baboon's grandfathers, uncles and distant cousins share the sense of guardianship. The German explorer Brehm, out with his hunting dogs, once came upon a troop of baboons that were playing near a rocky escarpment. The dogs rushed in and, as the baboons scampered up the cliff, cut off the retreat of one of their children. The little baboon climbed a big rock and perched there miserably, just out of

Family life among monkeys and apes shows many close resemblances to our own. Most intelligent of the apes are **chimpanzees,** which can be taught to imitate human behavior in a variety of ways. The father's role in raising the young chimpanzee begins after it is weaned, at which time he starts to play with it and protect it.

reach of the dogs' snapping jaws. A big old grandfather baboon saw what had happened. Without hesitation he came climbing resolutely down the cliff, and moved towards the rock. As he came he rapped a menacing thud-thud on the ground with his powerful hands, bared his teeth, and snarled such furious defiance that the dogs fell back before him. The old fellow climbed the rock, picked up the baby baboon, and carried him off to safety.

In recent years, many scientists have been working with monkeys, apes and other primates, and a great deal has been learned. Previously, all studies were made of animals in captivity, and almost the only way humans watched them in the wild was over the barrel of a gun. The modern method is for one or two persons to go into the jungle as unobtrusively as possible, and live with a colony until the animals come to accept the human presence without fear. This may take from several months to a year or more; but then, and only then, can the normal behavior of the wild creatures be studied at close range. Many species have been treated in this manner in the past few years, especially gorillas, baboons and chimpanzees. Mankind has learned much more in the past five or ten years, through the use of these methods and by using photographic equipment intelligently, than could possibly have been learned in any other way over a vastly longer period.

In a few places "wild" populations of monkeys and apes have become so used to man, and have not been molested, that some, at least, of their habits can be studied with ease. One example is the colony of rock apes, or Barbary apes that have lived on the Rock of Gibraltar for hundreds of years. They are actually macaques, and the only monkeys found wild in Europe; they were probably imported from South-east Asia long ago. Legend has it that so long as they live on the Rock, British will rule. Whatever the reason, they are tolerated, which is fortunate; there may be as few as thirty individuals left.

All marmosets are small—none larger than a grey squirrel—and in some species the young is barely five-eighths of an inch long. Interestingly, the father normally carries them, tucked away against his abdomen and pointing backward. They are given to the mother for nursing, then taken back again. Twins seem to be the rule.

Children of the Great Earth Family

THE STORY OF ANIMALS' CHILDHOODS is one of the most revealing stories we can learn outdoors. It may make us think about a lot of things. Perhaps most vividly, it may make us feel the oneness of all creation, the bond among all the many forms of life from humblest to highest. For we see that under the creative scheme of nature all of us, each in our fashion, each in our appropriate way of birth and growth and learning, as the great life of the world has been evolved, are really members of a single family of children.

(opposite page)
A **baby marsh hawk** or harrier has a big appetite, and during its first weeks of life the parents spend a good part of their time supplying it with food. The father does the hunting, while the mother stays near the nest, taking the food from him and dividing it among the young. Since the nest is on the ground, the parents are particularly careful to guard the chicks from any possible predators. After about a month the parents begin to teach the young birds to fly, gradually persuading them to fly higher. Finally, the young are taught to hunt and are made to leave the nest completely. Then they are on their own.

► *Coloring, shape, and other characteristics provided by nature to enable animals to survive in hostile environments.*

Camouflage in Nature

How to eat and not be eaten is a pressing problem in the natural world. To survive, non-vegetarians wage a continuous campaign against their own natural prey while relying on ingenious tricks and camouflage for protection against larger enemies.

In this primeval struggle there is a ceaseless armament race in which increased effectiveness in attack is countered by improved defensive techniques. Better streamlining brings increased speed in the air, on land, or in the water for pursuer and pursued alike. Both have perfected stealth and surprise; deception and ambush; traps, nets and parachutes; spears, spines, stings and fangs; poison and poison gas.

Over the thousands and thousands of years that our present-day animals have been evolving, there has been ample time and opportunity to try out and adopt (or discard) many different patterns of hue, habits, sizes, shapes and body forms. Competition for food and the presence of predators have become an automatic weeding-out process whereby those animals that were *least* efficient at catching their own food, hiding, running, flying or otherwise escaping, have been eliminated, leaving the *most* efficient to breed. So any camouflage pattern that proves itself to be successful tends to persist, by being passed down through the generations, and may even be refined and improved in the process.

In the refinements of "civilized" warfare man has fashioned a host of parallel inventions for protection, and for aggression. Many of them have now been developed to such an incredibly complex degree that they surpass the most fantastic contrivances of nature; yet in the sphere of concealment and deception nature has achieved a perfection that man can rarely equal.

Many animals rely on tricks and camouflage for protection against their larger enemies. (above, right) A **hawk-moth caterpillar** is also called a "sphinx moth" because it adopts this sphinx-like pose when alarmed. (above, far right) These two big "eyes" on the **caterpillar of the spicebush swallowtail butterfly** are not really eyes at all; they are nothing but spots of pigmentation. However, by making the head seem like that of a much larger animal, some possible enemies may be frightened away.

MEL HUNTER

For Centuries We Have Tried Our Hand at Camouflage

MAN'S EXPERIMENTS IN DECEPTION are by no means recent. Primitive hunters in many parts of the world have put on nature's disguises—often the skins of the very animals that they sought to approach, ambush, or allure. Such themes have been used a good deal in literature; the undetected advance of Malcolm's troops against Macbeth at Dunsinane, in Shakespeare's play, depended on the carrying of branches from the trees of Birnam Wood as camouflage.

But even man's more recent, elaborate efforts to disguise his military installations often seem feeble in comparison with nature's widespread and highly effective camouflage. If you have ever walked along a country road, through the woods, or across a stony field you have probably encountered some example of camouflage in nature.

Perhaps you have seen a meadowlark fly across the road, glide into a close-cropped hay field and instantly disappear; or a woodfrog repeatedly vanish as you pursued it through the dead leaves on the forest

(below)
Color adaptation is important for birds such as the **skylark,** which nest on the ground. With plumage that matches the colors of a field, a bird like this may land and disappear from sight.

(below)
Good camouflage may help to explain why reptiles such as this Everglades **alligator** survive today. Hundreds of other reptiles, including the enormous dinosaurs, have become extinct in the course of time.

floor. The frog will have been invisible except when it moved. A kill-deer may have been flushed from its nest of eggs among the pebbles of a dry stream bed as you almost stepped upon it without seeing it. You might even have been lured away from the nest by the injury-feigning act of the bird and then discovered, too late, that you could no longer locate its camouflaged eggs.

Each of these disappearing acts is an example of a basic principle of concealment. The "rules" are so universal that we find them followed by members of virtually every group of animals, in habitats of many types, and in all parts of the world. If we learn these basic rules we can sharpen our powers of observation and increase both our under-standing and our enjoyment of nature.

Most Creatures Resemble the Tint of Their Surroundings

THE COMMONEST METHOD of concealment is so familiar that we take it for granted. Subconsciously, we associate the white of the polar bear, the snowy owl and the arctic hare with the snow and ice of the far north. And we accept as natural the fact that a preponderance of green insects, tree toads, snakes and even greenish birds live among the green leaves of woodlands, that pale brownish grey creatures dwell in sandy deserts and dark brown ones on bare soil and mud flats.

Yet on the perfection of this kind of *background matching* the very existence of countless creatures depends. Even a slight difference be-tween the hue of an animal and that of its surroundings makes it more noticeable, and therefore more vulnerable to its enemies or less efficient in catching its own food. Actually, a multitude of animals show the closest possible resemblance between the tone and hue of their own bodies and that of the vegetation on which they live.

Southern green tree frogs, for example, hide by day in green air plants growing on the brown trunks and branches of trees. Even if they do not retreat almost out of sight into moist leaf-bases, they match

(top left)
Background matching is the commonest method of concealment. A green **frog** or a russet one on the grassy or muddy bank of a pond would be difficult to see unless it hopped.

(top right)
Hiding is easy for these **tree frogs,** whose pale green skin matches the coloring of many leaves.

the pale green of the fleshy leaves so perfectly as to be virtually invisible.

Various species of "horned toads", the flattened spiny lizards so characteristic of desert country, show remarkable variations which enable them to match the places in which they live. Some resemble the local rocks; others are uniformly grey ones to match the grey soil on which they are found. There is a very white horned lizard that lives on white alkali soil in the Amargosa Desert; others, from black lava beds, are themselves almost black. You can even find these lizards in a forest of California matching the brown carpet of pine needles.

Animals of Different Hues May Live Almost Side by Side

PALLID DEER MICE LIVE on sandy shores within sight of the shady redwood forests; within the forest itself another, dark, race of deer mice occurs. Each species is well concealed in its own surroundings. But if they were to change places neither race would stand much chance of survival.

On other areas of dry sand along seacoasts the pale piping plover and snowy plover make their nests; and for weeks on end, while they incubate their eggs, they set in full view of their enemies. They match their background perfectly, and when they leave their nests to feed, these plovers stay on the dry sand which they resemble. But the closely related ringed or semipalmated plovers frequent the *wet* sand whose darker brown is more like their own plumage.

Differences such as these can often be found within the same family of animals. The cats are a good example. Their markings are closely related to their environment. The snow leopard of the almost treeless steppes of central Asia is whitish, while the tree-inhabiting ocelot, the jaguar and the clouded leopard all have boldly marked patterns that suit the contrasting light and shade which is typical of forest interiors. The vertical orange and black stripes of the tiger match the grass

Often the coloring of different members of the same family of animals shows extraordinary variety, each matching the environment in which the particular species lives. The coats of foxes are a good illustration. Shown here are (extreme left) the **corsac** or **steppe fox** of Central Asia, (center left) the **arctic fox** in its white winter coat and (left) the **fennec** or **desert fox** of North Africa and Arabia.

stems and reeds of the swamps and grassy plains. The unstriped, unspotted American puma and African lion closely resemble the uniform light brown of the sandy and rocky areas they inhabit.

Even "Conspicuous" Marks Can Hide the Wearer

IF YOU HAVE WATCHED THESE BIG CATS in a zoo or in a circus or have looked at other conspicuously marked animals such as zebras and antelopes, you may have wondered how they possibly could avoid immediate notice and recognition. They would seem to be highly visible

The **bold black-and-white stripes** of a **zebra** are very noticeable in daylight, but when camouflage is most needed, at dusk and dawn, they merge with the grasses and shrubs very effectively. Even during the day this pattern provides a type of camouflage, disrupting the animal's outlines and making it difficult for a predator to determine which way it is heading.

even at a great distance. But big game hunters will tell you that *in their natural surroundings* tigers and zebras fade so completely into the pattern of their background that even the most keen-eyed and experienced native hunters frequently cannot see them at forty or fifty yards. Of course, in bright strong sunlight the bold patterns of these animals are certain to be prominent; their camouflage is most effective in the soft light of dawn and twilight, and on cloudy days. When the sun shines brightly the zebras will often congregate in the middle of an open plain—where they are highly visible, but where their enemies are visible too! Even if a predator is well camouflaged, his shadow will give him away; an undetected close approach is impossible.

How Immobility Helps the Hunted Animals

IN THE STRUGGLE FOR EXISTENCE both hunter and hunted benefit from their resemblance to the background, the environment in which they live. The hunted have an additional advantage of great value: by instinct and training they remain motionless in times of danger. Since most prey is detected either by its scent or by its motion, the majority of camouflaged creatures, like rabbits or woodcock, will escape at least temporarily if they "freeze". Many of them can remain as immovable as rocks for hours if necessary.

The hunter, on the other hand, cannot make such great use of the device of immobility; at some point he must take the initiative.

Living in the South American rain forests, **tinamous** such as this one can rely on their coloring to blend with the ground cover and dense vegetation. Remaining motionless will also help to conceal them.

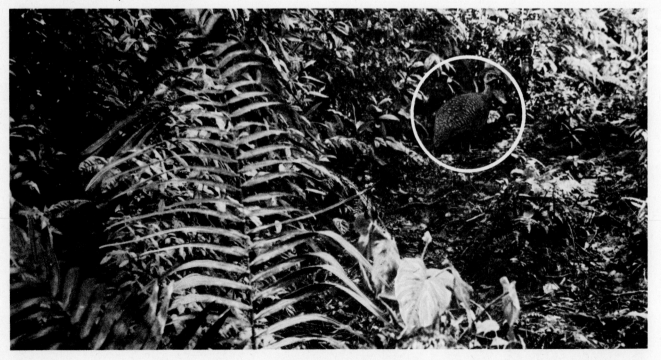

Most predators have three compensating advantages: they are camouflaged well enough to permit a stealthy approach to within striking distance of their prey; the sound of their advance is reduced or muffled; and they have no telltale scent.

A predator is thus well equipped to remain unrecognized until he can come dangerously close to his intended victim. Then—at the right moment—concealment is cast off; it is speed of attack that counts now! If the hunter catches the prey off guard, he eats; but if he has moved even a little too soon and so given warning of his attack he is likely to go hungry. The smaller animal may have moved enough to avoid, or at least to confuse, the predator and so make its escape.

(top left)
The young of many higher mammals wear special protectively-colored coats that often change when they grow up. Rows of white stripes and spots mark a **tapir** baby, but these are lost when it becomes an adult.

(top right)
A few birds and other animals can change their camouflage to match the changing background of different seasons. In winter, for example, the **snowshoe rabbit** of North America and the European **Alpine hare** exchange their brown fur coats for white ones.

A Young Fawn Can Disappear

SINCE MOST VERY YOUNG BIRDS and animals are unable to escape their enemies by precipitous flight, it is not surprising to find that they exhibit some of the most effective forms of "passive defensive" methods in existence. As an American white-tail fawn moves unsteadily around, its spotted coat may seem to be a dangerously conspicuous adornment; but when curled on the brown forest floor with its head lowered, the fawn disappears. The white spots blend neatly with the bright flecks of sunlight that filter down through the leafy woodland canopy. Furthermore, since the fawn, like most other young animals, has no scent, it can lie motionless and undetected all day long, well protected from prowling predators.

Even human eyes find the spotted fawn very hard to detect; predatory animals, which see only in "black and white", must have an even harder time of it. In the autumn of the year, a white-tail deer fawn loses its spots and becomes a uniform grey-brown. This serves as good camouflage, since the deer is standing most of the time by now and, in much of its range, the trees will have lost their leaves and the woods themselves are grey-brown.

Some Creatures Change Their Costumes to Suit the Seasons

MANY KINDS OF GREEN INSECTS blend with the greenery of their spring and summer surroundings. When the vegetation turns brown later in the year so do the carnivorous praying mantis, many grasshoppers and a host of other small plant-eaters.

The praying mantis needs camouflage so that insect-eating birds won't find him—and also so that small moths and other insects will come close enough so that *he* can catch *them*. The vegetarian, plant-eating insects need camouflage only for their own protection, so they will be relatively invisible while resting upon and eating leaves.

Some butterflies show well-marked differences between wet- and dry-season broods. Especially in the tropics, where the contrast between wet and dry seasons is most marked, different broods of butterflies may show modifications both in form and in hue. The dead-leaf butterflies and the famous Indian *Kallima* butterfly are good examples; the wet-season phase has a more conspicuous or "dazzling" pattern than the dry-season phase, which resembles the dead leaves to such an extent that the wings may be bent, in perfect imitation of the curled and warped leaves.

It is a well-known fact that many northern birds and mammals are white, or turn white as winter approaches. The polar bear, snowy owl, gyrfalcon and arctic hare are known to almost everyone, at least by reputation. In the extreme north the arctic fox nearly always discards its bluish-brown summer garb for a pure white winter coat; the Hudson Bay lemming also becomes white, while northern species of weasel turn white too, except for the black tips of their tails, and become the source of the coveted ermine fur.

Most interesting are birds such as the ptarmigan and mammals such as the snowshoe hare, whose changes have been closely studied. In summer, various species of ptarmigan in high mountains and in the far north have delicate brown patterns which enable them to escape

(above)
At all seasons of the year, the **ptarmigan** is hidden from its enemies by matching its background very closely. This summer plumage matches the rocks and gravel of the high mountain areas. It will gradually grow lighter as winter approaches, becoming completely white when everything is covered in snow.

(right)
Camouflage serves a double purpose for the **praying mantis.** It is a protection against insect-eating birds and it also hides the mantis from the insects that it feeds on. Waiting quietly on a green plant, the mantis may look perfectly harmless, but the moth or fly that comes too close may be caught and eaten.

A **stick insect** looks so much like a twig that it is probably mistaken for one in most instances. Indeed, unless it is seen moving against a background of a different color, who would think that it is really a living insect and not a piece of dead wood?

Despite what seems to be a noticeable pattern, this **butterfly** would be almost invisible on a lichen-covered or blotched tree trunk. To avoid being seen, such an insect must pick its backgrounds carefully.

notice even from a few yards away. So well do they blend with the shadowy pattern of the grasses, and so confident, seemingly, are the ptarmigan of their invisibility that they sometimes creep away while you are standing by watching them.

In autumn this bird's plumage begins to show areas of white. Since early snow flurries leave white patches on the landscape the bird's camouflage is obviously effective. As winter approaches and snow-storms are more frequent the ptarmigan becomes completely white. In spring the bird gradually develops its darker plumage, until by the time the snow has mostly disappeared the ptarmigan is brown once more.

How Those Changes Occur

O F COURSE, NEITHER THE FEATHERS of the ptarmigan nor the fur of the snowshoe rabbit actually "turn white". All birds and mammals "wear out" their coats and periodically grow new ones. Among many of the northern-dwelling creatures the new coat happens to be of a markedly different tone. The old fur or feathers are not shed suddenly and all at once, but gradually. During the transition a curiously "moth-eaten", mottled appearance results but it serves effectively to make the wearer inconspicuous in its changeable surroundings.

The seasonal molt also takes place among creatures in warmer latitudes and provides improved camouflage for many of them. Male ducks of many species shed their bright breeding plumage in midsummer and seem to melt into the background. They are flightless for a short time while their main wing feathers are being replaced. They would be almost completely at the mercy of any predator that might come across them during this period, but for one thing. They cannot fly away as they normally would do; but their dull "eclipse plumage" provides protective camouflage at a time when they most need it.

Some Deer Shed Their Spots, Others Keep Them

WE HAVE SEEN THAT A DEER FAWN has white spots that tend to conceal it among the tiny shafts of sunlight in the summer woods. The white hairs that make up the spots are replaced by brown ones as winter approaches. There are no leaves in the winter to cast a pattern of light and shadow, so a uniform coat is more protective. This might lead us to expect deer from warm countries, where there are leaves on the trees all year, to keep their spots all year. This is true of at least some such deer. The axis deer, or chital, of India and Ceylon, keeps its spots throughout its life, and is found in a great many different habitats. The barasingha of India has two rows of spots down its back, and retains these permanently. The fallow deer, so common in deer parks and zoos, is covered with spots which it loses in time for winter and which it recovers the following spring.

It seems that the deer of a single species that is found over a wide range tend to retain their spots in the warmer regions of it, where the trees keep their leaves; but there is much we cannot yet explain. There are herds of fallow deer that have a dark, unspotted appearance the year round; some bands of bighorn sheep contain both dark and

(bottom left)
Although most ptarmigan species exchange their summer plumage for a winter one of white, one species does not make the change: the **red grouse.** This bird, a native of the British Isles, keeps its same coloring the year round.

(bottom right)
Young **fallow deer** do not lose their spots permanently when winter comes but only until spring. Some herds of this species, however, are found to have dark, unspotted coats throughout the year. It is not always easy to tell if these differences are of advantage to the animal or not.

The Thompson's **gazelle** and some related species have horizontal dark-and-light stripings on their coats. When the animals are moving at great speeds, these markings may be confusing to a pursuer.

light individuals; some red squirrels develop a black line along their sides in summer, and their eartufts grow longer in winter. Are these changes of advantage to the animals? We can only guess at the answer.

Nature's Quick-change Artists

SWIFT CHANGES OF SHADE are possible in some of the "higher" animals, particularly among mollusks, fishes, amphibians and reptiles. Best known as a quick-change artist is the African chameleon and the American *Anolis* lizard. The latter is a familiar "circus souvenir"—but one which usually disappoints its purchaser. While it is capable of changing from pea green to dark brown, that is the limit of its repertoire. Even then its appearance seems to be influenced strongly by moisture, and to depend on the light falling on it.

This writer once found a half-dozen *Anolis* lizards hiding beneath a tin sign on a pine tree. In the darkness beneath the sign they had become pale green. Suddenly exposed when the sign was lifted they were spectacularly contrasted against the dark tree trunk. Yet within two or three minutes they turned a dark brown which perfectly matched

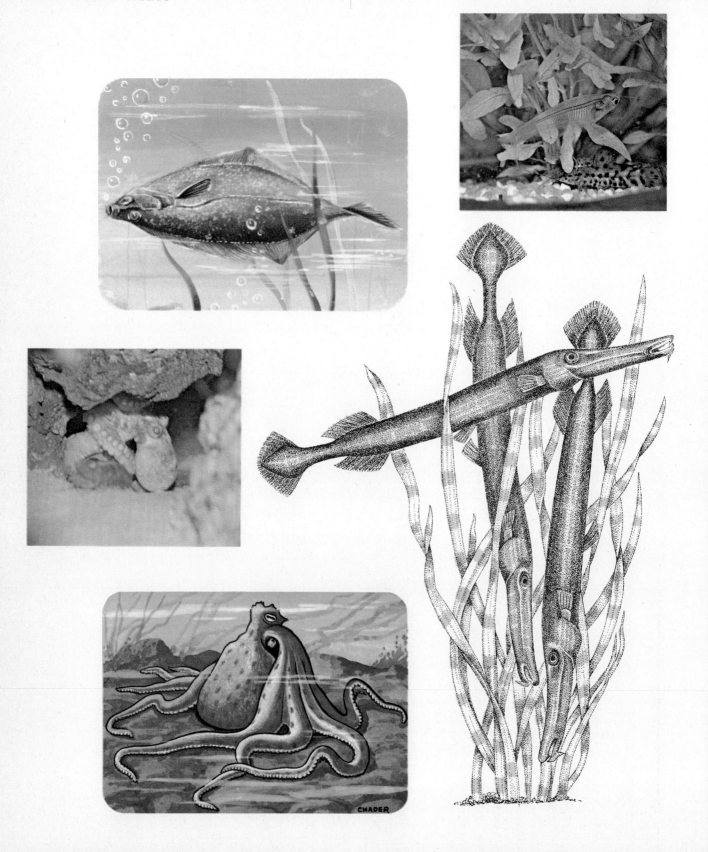

the bark. Anyone who has hunted for them knows that these lizards are masters at assuming poses which put them in line with stems and narrow leaves, making them very hard to spot.

Amazingly rapid changes are carried out underwater by the surgeonfish, the Nassau grouper, and various flatfish or flounders. The surgeonfish, for example, is mostly black when moving about among the coral reefs. But when it swims upward into clear water the fish quickly changes to a pure pale blue-grey of the very lowest visibility.

The Nassau grouper is one of dozens of reef fishes which can change its appearance more or less instantaneously in this way. The grouper can assume six, seven, or eight different "costumes" within a few moments. When a skin diver locates a grouper resting under a coral head, a slow approach may treat him to a display of the fish's entire "wardrobe". This fish is usually quite dark, with prominent bands, and will face the swimmer as soon as it sees him. Minor changes take place as the distance between them lessens, and the fish will usually erect its fins and back up slightly. Two or three different hues may appear and vanish. The fish may then come forward a few inches and make some grunting sounds; if this fails to frighten the swimmer away the grouper will abandon its refuge and swim rapidly to the next coral head or dark hole, turning almost white as soon as it is in the open. It often gives a whole series of indignant-sounding grunts at the same time! It is probably no coincidence that when frightened suddenly the Nassau grouper adopts a strongly banded appearance. This happens to be the most concealing of all its disguises, and works best among the strong shadows of corals and sea fans where this fish spends much of its time. Only the kaleidoscopic changes that sweep across the octopus and some of its cephalopod relatives surpass the swiftly-changing camouflage of some of the reef fishes.

opposite page:
(top right)
The best way to become invisible is to have a transparent body, which is what some fishes and shrimps have done. In the **glass catfish,** for example, only the bones, eyes and internal organs can be seen, and it is almost impossible to detect when it hangs motionless in the water of an aquarium.

(top left)
To an astonishing degree, a **flounder** can match the tint and even texture of almost any background. Its flat body also makes it possible for it to lie on the bottom without casting a shadow.

(center and bottom left)
A sort of underwater "chameleon," the **octopus** is able to change its hue rapidly to match its surroundings or to show emotion. Brown, black, red and white are often seen.

(bottom right)
Trumpet fish have to depend on adopting a suitable posture among their surroundings for camouflage. They normally swim horizontally, but when threatened they do a headstand among strands of sea plants or soft corals, even swaying with them in the currents.

(left)
Chameleons are the masters of rapid changes. They can assume the hues of dead bark or the green of growing leaves, taking poses that put them in line with the particular background. This species, from Madagascar, has two permanent stripes; others may have none.

Some Flounders Seem Able to Match Any Background

THE FAMILIAR FLOUNDER can vary from the palest sandy hues to a shade of deepest brown; it can be yellow—or even almost black. Generally it perfectly matches the tint of its background. Still more remarkable, it even simulates the appearance of the *texture* of the bottom on which it lies, whether mud, sand, or gravel.

Scientists have put the flounder's ability in this respect to the supreme test. They have placed one of these flatfishes in an aquarium with a glass bottom and then inserted beneath it various patterns, from finely stippled designs to bold polka dots and even a checkerboard. To an astonishing degree the flounder was able to alter its appearance to match that of its bizarre background. Needless to say, this must be a tremendous advantage in escaping notice when large hungry fishes are present. Not only can the flounder go almost anywhere in reasonable safety by matching its changing background: whenever it is not swimming it lies so flat against the bottom that it casts no shadow!

About the only way that an animal could improve on this technique would be by becoming completely transparent so as to achieve invisibility by letting the background show through. Though higher animals are unable to do this, a few of the fishes have managed it. The glass catfish is a common and popular aquarium fish. Nearly its entire body is almost perfectly transparent, and one can see rocks and plants right through it. Only the bones, eyes and internal organs are visible—and they seem to be as much reduced in size as possible. A few other species, with normal-sized viscera and non-transparent fins, are somewhat more conspicuous; these are very popular with youngsters, who can thus study the internal construction of a living fish without difficulty. The glass catfish spends most of its time hanging motionless in the water, usually pointing upward at a slight angle. This stillness makes the fish almost impossible to detect unless one knows more or less exactly where to look for it.

(bottom left)
Slow-moving and heavy-bodied, a Malayan **pit viper** waits for its prey to come along. Obviously, since it is important for this snake to remain unseen until its prey is very close, good camouflage is necessary if it is not to go hungry.

(bottom right)
Young **treefrogs** are often a bright green, which blends with the greenery of the woods. The adults, usually green, brown or grey, can change their hue to match the background, although this may take several hours.

A Uniformly Colored Object Is Not Invisible

A HAWK OR OWL FLYING directly over a white ptarmigan in the snow probably could not spot the bird; but an arctic fox, at ground level, might notice it. That is because the underside of the bird would be enough darkened by its own shadow to make it fairly easily seen from the side.

You can demonstrate this fact by putting a Ping-pong ball on a sheet of white paper and illuminating it strongly from directly above. The lower side of the ball will be shaded and its spherical shape is immediately apparent. Even a tennis ball painted green could be seen on a lawn because its shadow would make the lower portion look darker.

Counter-shading Is a Basic Principle of Camouflage

N ATURE HAS SOLVED THIS PROBLEM by distributing darker tones on the backs of animals, where light is strongest, paler ones on the sides which may be lightly shaded, and the palest underneath where shadows are darkest. The result is a tonal balance which reduces the visible solidity of the creature. It appears to be relatively flat, and far more likely to blend successfully against a similarly more or less plain background, such as snow or sand.

Any hunter can provide testimony of this. He has learned that when he turns one of his trophies *upside down* in the spot where he shot it, the carcass "stands out like a sore thumb". Yet turned right side up the natural gradation of tone provided by fur or feather is such that it almost perfectly neutralizes the effect of "shading" that would otherwise make the form so conspicuous. This kind of tonal shading is known as counter-shading or obliterative shading. It is of extremely wide occurrence in nature.

Even animals with stripes and other bold patterns exhibit counter-shading. At a distance the spots and stripes may blend, and as a rule they are boldest on the back and taper off as they go down the sides of the animal.

Counter-shading Works Well in the Water

S UCH GRADATION MAKES FISH of many species very hard to see from almost any angle. From the side they appear flat and unreal. From above, the back is difficult to recognize. It merges into the deep blue or leaden grey of the ocean depths or into the muddy or olive tones of the river bottom, or into the pebbly bed of a mountain brook. When, on the other hand, fishes are seen from beneath, as they sometimes are by their aquatic pursuers, their silvery undersides can be indistinguishable from the bright surrounding background of the sky unless directly silhouetted against it. It is not hard to understand why combat

(top)
Three rows of white spots decorate the tawny coat of the **roe deer fawn.** In addition to this protective coloring, the lack of a scent also helps the baby deer remain unnoticed.

(above)
If this **iguana** were unpatterned and had a smooth outline, it would stand out amid the palm fronds. As it is, the stripes and the spines along its back tend to mask its true shape.

airplanes are commonly camouflaged in this same way. Being darker on top, they are hard to see from above; silvery or white below, they tend to merge with sky above them.

It is significant that the remora or shark sucker lacks counter-shading. One can find an explanation for the omission in its habits. Since it is a hitchhiker on sharks and attaches itself without regard to the direction of light, counter-shading would offer no advantages and in some circumstances could well be a disadvantage.

Reverse counter-shading is found in the larvae of the eyed hawk moth. These caterpillars feed in an upside-down position; nature has provided for this! In this case the ventral surface, which is so often uppermost, is *darker* than the back. The result is such complete camouflage that insect collectors learn to look first of all for partly eaten leaves—and then to feel among them for the caterpillars. Sometimes it is easier to find them by touch than by sight.

The Telltale Appearance of Form Must Be Destroyed

THE FAMILIAR SHAPE OR SILHOUETTE of birds and mammals makes them quickly recognizable. Therefore any design which will serve to catch the eye and distract attention from the shape can have real survival value. Nature has developed some very effective means for obliterating the silhouette, and so "falsifying" the telltale form.

Good examples are the killdeer and its relative, the ringed plover. In each species the bird's body and part of its head are brown like the soil; but the head and body are separated by a boldly contrasting white neck with black rings above and below the neckband. The resulting visual impression is of something very different from the real physical shape of these creatures. The head is "optically chopped off" —and, if one notices these dabs of brown at all, the thought that they could "add up to a bird" may not even enter one's mind!

(bottom left)
A male **iguana** has a saw-toothed dewlap, or throat sack, under its throat. The **crest of soft spines** on the back, which stands out clearly in this picture, runs from one end of the body to the other.

(bottom right)
The **gecko** is one of the few lizards that regularly lives with man, but because of its natural camouflage it is seldom noticed. Geckos are great insect-eaters and for this reason they are usually welcomed.

In bright sunlight the strong patterns of a **giraffe** are very noticeable, but in the mottled shade it frequents, they blend with spots of sunlight and leaf shadows. In keeping with the principle of counter-shading, the spots are boldest on the back and taper off as they move down the giraffe's sides.

Counter-shading, the distribution of darker tones on the back of an animal and lighter ones on the underside, is a common camouflage device. Even at night, when the **black-backed jackal** hunts, its counter-shaded coat may help to conceal it from the hunter and its own prey. Notice the black back and reddish-brown flanks, which merge into white fur below.

THIS SCALY ARMADILLO
ROLLS ITSELF UP INTO
A TIGHT BALL OF TOUGH SCALES

THE PORCUPINE FISH
SWELLS UP LIKE A SPINY BALLOON

THE OPOSSUM
NATURALLY PLAYS "POSSUM"

THE BITTERN FREEZES
WITH ITS BILL POINTED UP

THIS GEOMETRID CATERPILLAR
HIDES BY RESEMBLING
ANOTHER TWIG

THE TREEHOPPER SETS
ITSELF UP TO RESEMBLE
A THORNY BRANCH

Regardless of their camouflage, various animals adopt special postures when danger approaches. Since movement is what gives so many animals away to their predators, "freezing" is one way of avoiding detection. When motionless, **treehoppers** and **geometrid caterpillars** appear to be thorns or twigs on a branch, while the vertical position of the **bittern** lets it blend with the reeds and cattails of a marsh. Trusting instinct, the **opossum** pretends to be dead and the **armadillo** rolls itself into an armored ball, but the cautious **sea snail** retreats into the security of its shell. An aggressive display may frighten some enemies away, and the fierce pose of the **frilled lizard** when its collar is spread may be all that is needed. Similarly, the **porcupine fish** has its own way of "looking tough," blowing itself up and erecting spines that can be unpleasant to any foe that pursues the matter further.

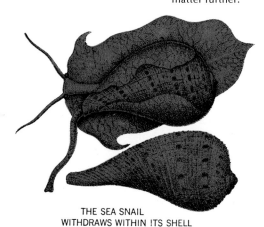

THE SEA SNAIL
WITHDRAWS WITHIN ITS SHELL

THE FRILLED LIZARD
EXPANDS ITS COLLAR FIERCELY

The Eye of the Observer Is Misled

MANY CREATURES HAVE A STRONGLY MARKED STRIPE, right down the back. A good many kinds of frogs and toads do, with the result that a potential enemy probably sees two half-frogs, which bear no resemblance to a whole one. If the brain behind the eye fails to join them together there is no recognition, and the creature remains unmolested.

Anyone who has chanced upon a patterned snake in its natural environment knows that it can be one of the most difficult of reptiles to spot. Not only does a distracting design repeatedly carry the eye away from the snake's outline, but the pattern often resembles the type of terrain on which the snake is commonly found; this frequently is a forest floor covered with dead leaves—and a dead-leaf pattern is a common one among snakes. The fer-de-lance and its relatives the bushmaster and rattlesnake all exhibit such patterns; and all are best concealed when they are motionless.

Strongly contrasting adjacent hues tend to distract the eye of the observer so that the outline of the animal is less easily recognized. And if one of these hues, such as the brown of the killdeer's back, matches one that also exists in the background, then it can seem to fade out completely while the other one stands out emphatically. Under such circumstances, a casual glance may reveal nothing more significant than a few apparently unconnected fragments with no resemblance to any living object.

A banded design that passes across the back of a grasshopper or frog often continues across the folded legs, helping to hide two ordinarily conspicuous parts—the big hind legs. Other creatures have stripes running the full length of the body and across the extended legs. This seems to be most effective in hiding the inhabitants of grassy places.

Nature Goes to Great Lengths to Conceal the Eye

IT IS NOT SURPRISING that one of the stripes that so many animals wear, sometimes the only stripe, should pass through the eye. For the staring eye is by far the most noticeable single feature, the "dead giveaway", in most creatures. It is very hard to conceal it completely, even among larger, bold designs. In some lizards, amphibians, and in certain large nocturnal birds such as owls and nighthawks, the eye can be concealed by eyelids which have the same protective hues as the rest of the body.

Experienced naturalists not only "freeze" when they find themselves close to a wild bird or animal; they also squint, reducing the "warning eye" to an innocent slit which seems to reassure wary wildlife. Among insects, amphibians, reptiles, fishes, birds and mammals we find many species exhibiting prominent eye-stripes that cross the pupil or the

At rest, the **Io moth** and the **Caligo moth** (below) may look similar in appearance to the bark of a dead tree branch. When disturbed, however, they expose their hindwings (right), which have large eyespots that could be mistaken for the eyes of an owl or other large animal. While this is simply bluff, an attacking predator might be sufficiently startled and frightened away.

(above)
The wings of a **pine hawk moth** bear a close resemblance to the bark of the tree on which it is found.

whole eye and extend past it on both sides. The raccoon and badger are probably the best-known examples, but there are many more. Most swimmers in tropical seas have noticed the little butterfly fish, whose eye is hidden by a vertical dark stripe that resembles a blade of eelgrass.

In some, like the roseate tern, the whole top of the head is black and the bird not only appears to be eyeless, it seems to lack a head and therefore may remain completely unrecognized even at fairly close range. Such a disguise has obvious advantages; but other patterns may seem to our untrained eyes to be "all wrong".

The badger and ratel, or "honey badger", have black underparts and greyish backs. This is, of course, the exact opposite of the common "counter-shading" so often seen in nature. Part of the answer may lie in the fact that these are burrowing animals that spend a good deal of time in holes in the ground, and it may be that as they stand in the entrance of a burrow their black underparts merge with the darkness behind them. More to the point, probably, is the value of this bold pattern as a warning device. Badgers have courage, tenacity, strong claws and teeth, and can spray an offensive musk. Few animals will molest them if they recognize them, and a "quick-identification label" avoids discomfort for all parties concerned.

Background-picturing Produces Invisibility

SOME ANIMALS REPRODUCE on their bodies a surprisingly faithful picture of the details of their environment. This may consist of grasses or reeds, bark or lichens, coral or seaweed. The sargassum fish is a good example of such background-picturing. Living in the Sargasso Sea—that huge aggregation of seaweed that floats in the north Atlantic —the fish has weedlike extensions on its fins, and when motionless it is hard to spot.

Many ground-nesting birds have a similar kind of pattern, which might be said to be realistic rather than disruptive, and which disguises contrast with the birds' background which would otherwise be glaringly obvious. A very good example is the woodcock, which is all but undetectable when it sits on the ground. And sit it does!—one can almost literally step on an incubating woodcock before the bird will take flight; it makes the best possible use of its natural appearance by assiduously avoiding any movement that would betray its presence.

The sloth does not have to exert itself to match its background, but simply hangs under a branch in its usual manner, and lets its shaggy covering of hair blow and tumble about it as it will. The sloth's movements are so slow as to be hardly noticeable, and it has a further advantage in that algae grow in its coat, giving it a greenish cast that blends with that of the tree canopy.

Another interesting example is the caterpillar stage of various moths which feed upon and live among the needles of pine trees. They wear "pinstriped" suits, with stripes whose width and greenness closely match the pine needles!

So-called *cryptic resemblances* of this kind are largely confined to animals which are restricted to a very specialized habitat or to a very limited variety of food plants, resting places, or breeding sites. For it to be of maximum value the animal must, of course, be suitably posed; the striped caterpillar would make itself conspicuous if it moved at right angles to the pine needles. But cryptically marked species seem to react properly to visual cues around them and position themselves so that their patterns line up with their backgrounds.

(bottom left)
Patterned snakes like this **rattlesnake** have distracting designs that tend to lead the eye away from the snake's outline, making it difficult to see. The dead-leaf pattern also resembles a forest floor or other ground cover on which the snake may be lying quietly, waiting for its prey to draw near.

(bottom right)
The plumage of many ground-nesting birds, such as the **woodcock,** reproduces the details of their environments. When sitting completely still, a woodcock usually blends so perfectly with the ground that it is impossible to detect.

In Wartime, Camouflage Saves Lives

Background-picturing has been effectively adapted to the demands of modern warfare, most notably in the designing of the "jungle suit". The garment's strange-looking, irregular assortment of tan, green and dark brown spots is a realistic rendering of the shadow patterns that can be seen in the leafy jungle. When combined with the use of grease paint or other "cosmetics" to darken the wearer's face, the result is astonishingly good—in a jungle setting, of course. Another effective trick is to fasten leaves, twigs and grasses to helmets covered with netting designed for this purpose.

Less effective has been the unrealistic disruptive or dazzle painting designed to lead the eye away from the all-too-revealing outlines of buildings, military installations and ships. Developed in World War I, this kind of camouflage often fell short of what was required, mostly for sheer lack of the very boldness with which nature goes about the task. In part, too, even the best attempts at such methods of concealment can be spoilt by the effect of shadows—as we shall see later.

Aerial photography with infrared film which distinguishes between the green of chlorophyll and non-living green pigments has made camouflage an increasingly difficult art. Nowadays there are special films which make the difference between living vegetation and freshly cut foliage show up quite conspicuously and which are capable of even more sensitive "sorting" of the elements of the landscape, and so still further complicate man's efforts at concealment. And it is scarcely necessary to add the further note that radar is no more confused by visual camouflage than is a keen-scented predator that has really "ranged in" on its prey.

Very recently, specialized techniques using infrared radiations make it possible for a low-flying aircraft to scan the ground and take a "heat picture"—showing all sources of heat within view, *including*

(bottom left)
It is difficult to conceal the eye completely, but the two bright eyes of the **raccoon** are well hidden in a band of black fur, which gives this animal its famous "masked" appearance.

(bottom right)
The distinctive pattern of the **ratel** or **honey badger**—black underneath and much lighter on its back—may be a combination of camouflage and warning device. On the one hand, it may make it less noticeable as it stands at the entrance of a burrow; on the other, it cautions other animals to leave it alone or take the consequences.

(left)
Ground-nesting birds must rely on background-matching to protect themselves and their eggs from predators. It would be very easy to miss this **nest of the New Zealand oyster-catcher.**

If a **woodcock** moved, the dead-leaf camouflage pattern of its feathers would be of little use for concealment. When necessary, however, this bird can sit motionless for hours.

warm-blooded animals. Even a man hiding under a growing tree or bush, and thinking himself completely concealed, is not immune to this sort of spying.

Homes Are Often Hidden by Animal Architects

THE LARVA OF THE CADDIS FLY does not develop a body pattern that resembles its background as many insects do; it *manufactures* one! Living on the bottom of streams and ponds, these aquatic creatures gather up bits of bark and weave them together into a tube. Then they live inside this cylinder until they are ready to rise to the surface and change into airborne insects. Some species build structures of pebbles or sand grains, depending on the materials typical of their selected habitat.

A good many birds also use building materials which serve to hide or camouflage their homes. Phoebes, for example, often build their nests under mossy, overhanging cliffs, and work moss into the surface of the nest. The blue-grey gnatcatcher and the ruby-throated humming-bird gather lichens and camouflage their nests so well with these flat ashy green plants that the final result appears to be merely a bump or knot on a lichen-covered branch. So strongly implanted is the instinct to build like this that they cover the nest with lichens even if the branch happens to be a bare one! Though it is very noticeable then, at least the materials used are natural and common ones. Birds will often select nest-building materials that blend with or resemble the location in which they are building; they will not scorn to use man-made materials if they are suited to their purpose. It is not too uncommon to see paper tissues or paper napkins woven into a bird's nest, especially if it is built in a tree which has light bark. Birds will

(right)
A **sloth** always moves so slowly that it rarely gives its position away. A shaggy coat of pale, neutral hair, which blows about in the wind and often has algae growing in it, helps it to avoid notice as it hangs from the branches of the treetops in which it lives.

(below)
Although the color of this **lizard** closely matches that of the soil, its shadow could enable another animal to detect its presence. To avoid this, it crouches flat against the ground.

readily use string and ribbon for building, but, interestingly, they avoid more gaudy specimens when offered a choice. They seem to know instinctively that duller ones will make a better-camouflaged nest.

How Do You Get Rid of Your Shadow?

A SHADOW-LIKE PATTERN MAY HELP to conceal many forms of wildlife, but real shadows can reveal the presence even of perfectly counter-shaded creatures. The more uniform the background, the more conspicuous a shadow cast by an animal is likely to be. In the desert and on the beaches most animals reduce their shadows by crouching down close to the sand; they may even go so far as partly to bury themselves! Some lizards can expand their bodies sideways and downward until they touch the ground and therefore cast no shadow at all under a high sun.

Even more irregular outlines are found on some caterpillars such as the strangely fringed one that develops into the hag moth. The shadows cast by such creatures lack a familiar animal-like shape and often pass quite unnoticed.

Butterflies, like sailboats, could easily cast long conspicuous shadows; but by heading in the direction of the sun they can avoid making more than a thin line of a shadow. There are some butterflies, however, which rest at right-angles to the sun; but you will notice that these tip over enough to reduce greatly the length of the shadow they cast. Naturalists have noted that when approached these butterflies will tip either right or left, depending on the direction of the sun, and that this reaction is more consistent in sunshine than in shady surroundings.

It has already been mentioned that efforts to conceal buildings from aerial observation can be wasted because of the casting of revealing shadows, both in sunshine and in the glow of the tremendous flashes of light used in aerial photography at night. The best solution to the shadow problem is that which is demonstrated by the hag moth and the lizards mentioned above—that of extending "flaps" or screens outward and downward to break up or reduce the shadows which are characteristic of the "natural" outline. In recent years man has learned from nature and applied the method to buildings, railway cars, radar domes, gun emplacements, bridges, missile launchers, etc.

Some Creatures Trust Their Instincts More than Their Senses

A WIDE VARIETY OF ANIMALS instinctively and instantly adopt the most effective pose for concealment when danger threatens. As a rule the "freezing" position fits the setting. The bittern can often be seen in surroundings which offer somewhat less concealment than the reeds or cattails in which it normally lives. But anyone can appreciate how difficult it is to see the bird against such a vertically striped background, when it points its bill straight up at the sky.

This wonderful power of self-effacement of a marsh bird in danger first baffled and then intrigued the famous writer-naturalist, W. H. Hudson. After searching fifteen minutes for a heron which he thought he had wounded, he discovered it less than a foot away, standing like "a straight tapering rush". When Hudson tried to circle behind the heron he discovered that the bird turned, slowly or quickly as needed, to keep the narrow edge of its bladelike body toward him. Wondering whether the bird might be wounded or paralyzed by fear, Hudson placed his hand on the point of its beak, and forced its head down. When he withdrew his hand, up flew the head like a steel spring, to its first position. No matter how often the experiment was repeated the bird's head swung directly back to the rigid, upright position, its eyes unwinking.

It is worth noting that the bird instinctively presented its narrowest aspect in time of danger. Under similar circumstances other animals

(bottom left)
Protected by its coat and a thick layer of fat, the **honey badger** pays little attention to the bees whose honey it steals. Its claws are powerful enough to tear open a termitarium, and it also has strong teeth, courage, and an offensive musk it can spray. Other animals do well to take the bold grey-and-black pattern of its fur as a warning to keep away.

(bottom right)
Reddish brown in summer, the **snowshoe rabbit** has a white coat in winter and grows extra hair on its feet to help it travel on the snow. It is the main prey of the Canada lynx.

(right)
With its flat tail and fringes along its hind legs, the **leaf-tailed gecko** can blend almost perfectly with a mottled branch simply by lying flat against it. It casts less of a shadow than those lizards which lack these features.

will sometimes intimidate their enemies by enlarging themselves, just as certain birds and mammals do when they posture in front of rival males or members of the opposite sex. And sometimes a wild creature will do both—first trying to escape detection; then, if this is unsuccessful, making itself look as large and fierce as possible.

How Often Can a Snake Die?

THE SAME BLIND ACCEPTANCE of instinct seems to govern the hog-nosed snake, or puff adder, when its impressive but toothless bluff has been called. It rolls over and "plays dead" so convincingly that even its slender forked tongue hangs motionless from its mouth.

But let anyone pick up the "dead" snake and turn it right side up, and it flops right over on its back again. Since the underside of the snake has a much more striking pattern than the upper surface,

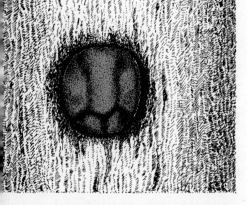

(above and right)
A few insects use their own bodies to camouflage their homes. The **janitor ant,** for example, blocks the entrance of its nest with its enlarged head, except when another ant is entering or leaving.

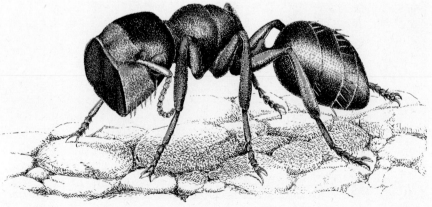

some naturalists believe that potential enemies may be warned off by the sight of it.

Camouflage Doesn't Always Work

W E HAVE DISCUSSED MANY EXAMPLES of animals which through certain adaptations of pigmentation, form and habits are extremely hard to recognize or even to detect in their natural surroundings. It must be understood, of course, that well-concealed animals are by no means immune from attack. Their capture may eventually result from their movement or from their scent, neither of which can be effectively eliminated. But scientists have demonstrated on many occasions that camouflage is a definite advantage. Mortality of experimental animals is consistently greater when they are exposed to enemies in surroundings which make concealment or camouflage impossible. And even slight advantages are important over the enormous period of time that is required for animals, through numerous generations, to develop a strain completely adapted to its environment.

What About Creatures Which Are Conspicuous?

E VERYONE KNOWS that not all creatures fade into their backgrounds. Camouflage seems to be unnecessary to big carnivores, such as bears, which have almost no enemies and which do not depend on stealth when approaching their prey. It seems unimportant to birds like herons, egrets and ibises which find safety in numbers and in the isolation of their colonies. It would be valueless to true cave dwellers; denizens of the dark abysses of the deep sea likewise need no concealment, though it is interesting that many of them are red; this apparently makes them hard to see in the near-darkness of the ocean depths. When there is no light at all, of course, all non-luminescent creatures are equally invisible, irrespective of their real hue.

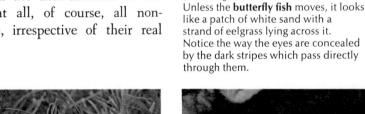

(bottom left)
The bold markings of a **tiger** may actually be good camouflage in its natural surroundings, especially at dawn and dusk. Since the tiger has almost no enemies, its camouflage serves not for its own protection but rather to help it escape notice as it stalks its prey.

(bottom center)
When a **bittern** is alarmed, it points its bill straight up at the sky. The stripes on its breast are then plainly visible, providing a good imitation of the surrounding reeds.

(bottom right)
Unless the **butterfly fish** moves, it looks like a patch of white sand with a strand of eelgrass lying across it. Notice the way the eyes are concealed by the dark stripes which pass directly through them.

But there are certain creatures notable for their conspicuousness. Many of them are vivid—with reds, oranges and yellows. Others have patterns so definite as to be unmistakable. And whereas well-concealed creatures generally have weak defensive equipment for use against attackers, the brightly or boldly marked ones usually are well able to defend themselves—with stings, as the bees and wasps; poison, as the snakes; unpleasant taste, in the case of many insects; or a repellent scent as with some other insects (and the skunk).

As a matter of fact, nature, after eons of experimentation, seems to have evolved a "system of marking" which ensures fair warning of danger being given to potential victims. For example, yellow and black, which have been adopted by man as a "warning badge", have a similar signification in the world of nature. Yellowjackets and hornets, bees and certain rattlesnakes display the same yellow and black combination employed for many of the standardized warning signs that can be seen on our highways, airports and construction sites.

"It Pays to Advertise"

SCIENTISTS HAVE DISCOVERED by studying insect-eating birds that the least acceptable insects, from among the 5,000 used, were those bearing conspicuous markings of red, orange, or yellow. Furthermore, among those which proved *most acceptable* to the birds tested, there was *not one species* which displayed these "warning" pigments when in the resting attitude in which they were seen by the birds. It can hardly be doubted, then, that "it pays to advertise". Young birds and other animals evidently learn to recognize such dangers largely by experience—and they learn fast!

Once predators have learned to avoid a certain animal because of unpleasant consequences it is likely that others with a similar appearance will be left alone too. Thus those creatures that "mimic" dangerous or distasteful ones have an advantage over those that look harm-

(above)
This Norwegian **brambling** has found an excellent method for hiding its nest—it has used white tissue as a building material and chosen a white birch tree as the site. It is not unusual for birds to select nest-building materials that blend with or resemble the location of their nests.

(right)
One must take a close look to tell a **hummingbird moth** from a hummingbird; their forms are similar and each hovers in front of flowers, sucking nectar through a long tongue.

lessly edible. One might ask why we say that an insect "mimics" another, when its appearance is something over which it has no control. This is a valid point, and has been the source of many arguments and discussions. When one creature *deliberately poses and acts* like another, it is another story altogether. We find this situation many times in the natural world. All spiders have eight legs; some species hold the two front ones up like antennae, giving themselves a close resemblance to ants—which have only six legs. Many moths look a great deal like wasps and hornets and act rather like them, too, which heightens the illusion. The hummingbird moth hovers before flowers like a hummingbird, so that even humans are often deceived.

Beware! They Are Defiant and Formidable

THE STRONGLY MARKED YELLOW-AND-BLACK TIMBER SNAKES and diamondback rattlesnakes and the beaded lizard are in no hurry to get out of danger's way. Nor is the unique, venomous Gila monster;

The coloring of many animals, such as the **bittern** (top left), helps them to blend with their backgrounds, especially when they do not move. On the other hand, certain animals have bright, vivid colors that are clearly visible. In general, yellow and black markings and other bold patterns may serve as a system of "fair warning" to other animals. **Yellowjackets** and **hornets** (top right and above, left), for example, whose stings make effective weapons, display the same warning colors that man has adopted for signs. An exception is the **death's head hawk moth** (above, right), which is not really to be feared in spite of its strange markings. In this case, however, it can benefit from the usual significance of this color scheme and be left alone by some of its more powerful enemies.

these big lizards are especially sluggish, whereas almost all other members of the reptile order to which they belong are extremely quick. This fact at least gives one a chance to recognize them before an attack actually takes place.

The orange and black blister beetle expels an acrid fluid; the monarch butterfly has a similar pigmentation and carries the unpleasant taste of the plant on which it feeds—the milkweed. The viceroy butterfly looks so similar to the monarch that it enjoys an immunity earned for it by the bad taste of the creature it so closely resembles.

Plenty of similar examples could be given; but the majority seem to fall into the "universal" black-and-yellow category which usually means "Danger—stay away". The more clearly an animal advertises its inedibility, or its potentially dangerous nature, the more likely it is to avoid being subjected to "accidental" attacks. This helps to avoid unpleasantness all round!

Is the Bright Color of Male Birds a Warning?

IT IS A WELL-KNOWN FACT that when both sexes of birds share the nesting duties, and incubate their eggs in exposed situations, the plumage of both sexes is inconspicuous. But brightly marked male birds usually keep at a distance from the nest, and this is apt to be well concealed; among such divergently plumaged pairs, the female is usually an excellent example of "background-picturing". The males are thought to direct the attention of natural enemies from the nest by their conspicuous livery.

Of course, a male's bright plumage serves other purposes also. Like his song, his plumage may help attract a mate or deter a rival. In some animals conspicuous exhibition of some distinctive feature—like the flash of the deer's white tail—may be a signal to other members of the herd. The "dichromatic" bills of colonial birds such as gulls, terns and some herons seem to serve as a target or "releaser" for the feeding response of the young and to be essential to their successful feeding. When adult herons and egrets bring fish and other food to the nestlings they are enabled to regurgitate it as a result of the young birds' instinctively grasping the parents' beaks *at just the right point*.

Some Warnings Are Reserved for Special Occasions

WHETHER USED IN COURTSHIP OR DEFENSIVELY many vivid markings are displayed only when really needed. As a rule, male lizards carry brightly pigmented patches on the throat and undersides. When they rear up suddenly they become so glaringly conspicuous that the sudden effect can be quite startling. As already pointed out, many creatures supplement this visual warning with strong reminders to their enemies' sense of smell. Some of them reinforce their warning

Even if the adult insects are well camouflaged, a species could be in danger if its eggs were easily noticed and laid where predators could readily find them. Many eggs are concealed, therefore, and often they have disguising markings as well. These **katydid eggs** are hidden on the underside of a twig.

with audible challenges—for example, by hissing, rattling, snorting or by pawing the ground.

Certain salamanders, like the newts of both Europe and America, writhe around and expose the bright pigmentation of their undersides if attacked. Toads often swell up when in danger; the sudden increase in size doubtless intimidates some enemies. Both the toads and newts back up the warning; poisonous secretions from the skin glands of some species are potent enough to kill a dog that attempts to eat one. Other creatures have to rely on bluff or intimidation alone. Some snakes exhibit their bright undersides when threatened; or they may bury their heads, and wave the headlike tail in the air as if to fool the predator into thinking *it* is the head. This at least deflects the attack from the highly vulnerable head to a less vital part of the body.

Disconcerting and impressive as these warnings may be, they occasionally fail to protect their possessors. Sometimes a scarcity of other food will force predators to settle for relatively unpalatable prey. And some birds, such as cuckoos, are specialists at catching tent caterpillars—while flycatchers regularly dine on stinging insects. But as a rule the advertisements serve their apparent purpose—they are respected as indicators of *something to be avoided*.

Some Warnings Are Nothing but Bluff

WHEN THE CATERPILLARS of certain swallowtail butterflies display huge "eyespots" on the head it is pure deception. They have nothing to back up the visual suggestion that they are much bigger and more dangerous than we know them to be. Other species may rear up, whether or not they exhibit eyespots, and may raise the rear end as well, if it is adorned with one or a pair of spines. One can hardly be surprised that these creatures seem to make full use of whatever bluff techniques they can master; mostly, they have virtually no other method of defending themselves.

The hog-nosed snake, when approached, spreads a hood created by the ribs on its topmost vertebra, and hisses ominously. But it never opens its mouth like the genuinely dangerous moccasin snake; and when its bluff fails to frighten its enemies the hog-nosed snake will turn over and feign death instead of trying to bite with its tiny but numerous teeth. All twelve species of cobras employ a similar defensive technique. They too spread a hood and hiss loudly; but they are well equipped, and ready, to deliver a poisonous bite when necessary.

How an Insect Gets That "New Look"

IN SOME ANIMALS the disguises involve deceptive markings. The characteristic narrow waist of a wasp is achieved in some plump,

(above)
These **least bitterns,** just out of the nest, already show the characteristic "hiding" posture, with their bills pointed up. Even without the stripes of the adult plumage, this helps conceal them among the reeds.

To remain unnoticed, an insect like this must stay around green leaves, where **background matching** will help conceal it. On a bare branch or tree bark it would certainly be in danger.

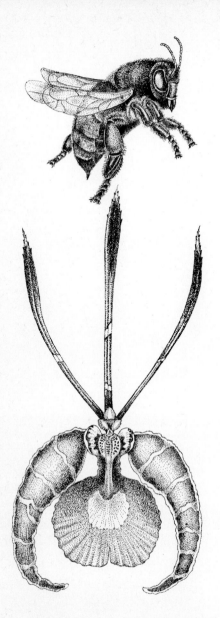

WASP OR BEE ORCHID

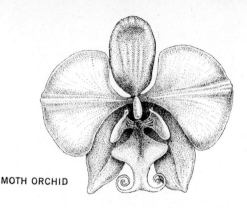

MOTH ORCHID

Through centuries of evolution, several species of **orchids** have come to bear a strong **resemblance to certain insects.** Some of them look very much like butterflies, moths, wasps, bees or even spiders.

non-stinging insects by contrast-camouflage on the waistline which reduces it, visually, to near-vanishing point. One Brazilian grasshopper with normally long antennae mimics a "short-horned" burrowing wasp in an ingenious way. The basal third of each long antenna is thickened like a wasp's, strongly ringed and banded with yellow. The remaining two-thirds suddenly narrows to the usual hairlike thinness. The deception is extremely convincing; the grasshopper really looks like a wasp.

A parallel example is the wartime disguise of certain naval vessels. Unlike the rather unsuccessful dazzle or obliterative painting used so much in World War I, this type of camouflage involved "painting out" key features—one of the stacks, or the telltale prow of the ship. Sometimes false superstructures were added, all to mislead the enemy as to the true type and size of the vessel.

Certain caterpillars which feed on bright flowers bite off fragments of the petals and fasten them to their own "superstructure". A nearly identical procedure is carried out on the sea bottom by various crabs that attach bits of seaweed, debris and even living anemones to their backs and carry them around. Since the anemone can sting, it offers its host more than passive protection on occasion. The anemone is repaid when the crab feeds, because the water around the crab then becomes filled with food scraps which the anemone catches and eats.

Protection of the eggs, and of the female bagworm, is probably increased by the insect's habit of decorating its cocoon with needles from the coniferous or evergreen trees in which it lives. The bag serves also as an egg case.

All day long the brown caterpillars of many kinds of moths stand rigid, looking so much like twigs that they even have irregular bumps and a head that resembles a bud. Some of them rest in this awkward position supported by a virtually invisible thread thrown around the twig. They feed at night.

Now You See Me, Now You Don't

MANY COMMON BIRDS DISPLAY BRIGHT MARKINGS prominently when they are in flight. These include "field marks" such as the conspicuous white outer tail feathers of meadowlarks and juncos—

features which offer the birdwatcher his best clues for quick identification. On the wing, one North American woodpecker, the flicker, flaunts a big white rump patch. A pursuing hawk whose gaze is fixed on this field mark may be confused when the bird lands, and the conspicuous mark instantly disappears. It becomes hidden beneath the cryptically marked wings or tail. An enemy in swift pursuit would almost certainly speed by the spot where the bird landed, and where it now is "freezing"

The same technique is used by many grasshoppers and by moths such as the Io, and various other underwing moths. Their camouflaged upper wings conceal lower wings that are often vividly marked. When disturbed in the daytime they take flight and instantly attract attention with their target-like lower wings. But, like the birds mentioned above, the moths simply vanish when they land on surfaces against which their quickly folded upper wings are equipped with almost perfect camouflage.

Conversely, if a bird should disturb a resting moth, it would doubtless be startled by the sudden appearance of the brightly-marked underwings—possibly long enough for the insect to fly around to the far side of the tree trunk, alight and "disappear" again.

Bright patches or eyespots on the wings of flying insects are usually near the outer edges. The frequency with which such insects can be seen to have tattered wings is evidence of the fact that such markings lure attacking birds into biting at parts far removed from vital organs. It is hard for humans, with no real enemies (except other humans), to appreciate the value of anything which seems so relatively unimportant; but in all of the non-human natural world the struggle for survival is so keen that a slight feature like this can determine the survival or disappearance of an entire species, and has done so.

(below, left)
The **false eyespots** make this **elater beetle** look more menacing than it really is. If molested, it can "click" itself several inches into the air. This action will also set it right again if it falls onto its back.

(below)
A **screech owl** on a branch may escape detection by squinting its eyes, flattening its feathers and holding itself tall and slim. If this fails and it is discovered, it will puff itself up and open its eyes wide, to make itself appear as fierce and dangerous as possible.

Again, we have a parallel situation in the sea. Just as the butterfly causes a diversion, the squid's smoke screen creates a similar state of confusion among its pursuers. So does the luminous discharge of certain shrimp that live at great depths in the ocean. The distraction often lasts long enough to permit the intended victim to escape.

It's Better to Lose a Little than to Lose All

MANY LIZARDS, AND SOME AMPHIBIANS such as the four-toed salamanders sacrifice a portion of their body to distract an enemy from more vital parts. Their long, thin tails are easily severed, sometimes voluntarily, and the wriggling appendage usually keeps the pursuer occupied until the now tailless animal has made its escape.

Escape, of course, is the purpose for much of nature's varied assortment of disguises. Hiding successfully can be vitally important, and, as we have seen, camouflage also enables many creatures to approach near enough to their prey for a successful surprise attack. Nature's camouflage is so universally used that no one can doubt its advantage to the wearer.

It is altogether too easy to pass by, unnoticing, many of the fascinating examples of how wild creatures live and compete with one another for food and living space. Having once seen and understood a few examples of how animals use camouflage to advantage, one cannot help but grasp a further and fuller knowledge of this fascinating field. "Knowledge breeds knowledge"; our new awareness makes us more alert, and we find more and more examples on every hand. It might even cause us to wonder why we didn't recognize them long ago. From now on each journey that we make to observe the natural world—be it a backyard jaunt or a long-distance safari—will yield a richer reward.

Even a very hungry grazing animal wouldn't try to eat a stone; so the **stone cactus** is often left alone when other green plants, easily recognized as food, are eaten down to the ground.

CREDITS
Color photographs and illustrations appearing in this volume were supplied by the following: Photo Researchers, Inc.; The American Museum of Natural History; Armando Curcio; Doubleday & Company, Inc.; U.S. Department of the Interior, National Park Service; and H. S. Stuttman Co., Inc.

Cover illustration and illustrations on pages 36-37 and 52-53 were photographed at The American Museum of Natural History.